The War Within

Dancing Through Psychosis

Second Edition

Jennifer Yi

Second Edition
This memoir is a work of nonfiction and reflects the author's personal experiences. Some names, identifying details, and events have been changed to protect the privacy of individuals. The author is not a medical professional, and nothing in this book should be considered medical advice. Readers should consult qualified professionals regarding health, mental health, or any medical concerns.

This memoir reflects what psychosis looked like for me. Everyone's experience is unique, and my story shouldn't be used to define anyone else's journey.

Dedication

To the ones who broke down and thought it meant they were broken. To the ones who saw visions no one believed. To the ones who heard voices, felt too much, loved too hard, or stayed silent because the world wasn't ready for their truth, this is for you.

To the girl I used to be, curled up in hospital beds, whispering prayers through tears, thinking she had lost her mind... You didn't lose anything. You were just waking up.

To my son, you were my reason to keep breathing when the world went dark. This book is a love letter to you, proof that your mama fought hard to come back whole.

And to anyone holding this book with shaking hands: I see you. You're not too much. You're not alone. You're not lost. You're just on your way back to your real self. Welcome home.

Contents

Dedication iii

Prologue: The Girl Who Danced with Demons viii

Chapter 1 - Grandiose, God, and I 1

Chapter 2 - The Universe Inside Me 2

Chapter 3 - The Day She Screamed 3

Chapter 4 - The Poltergeist 4

Chapter 5 - Hear No Evil, Say No Evil, See No Evil 5

Chapter 6 - The Chanting Sisters 7

Chapter 7 - Behave or Else 8

Chapter 8 - What the Mind Remembers 10

Chapter 9 - City Lights 11

Chapter 10 - I Didn't Get Pancakes Either 13

Chapter 11 - The Devil All Around Us 14

Chapter 12 - I'm Not a Fighter 16

Chapter 13 - The Devil Inside 17

Chapter 14 - Beneath the Long Sleeves 18

Chapter 15 - The Tell in My Hands 19

Chapter 16 - Pain Displacement 20

Chapter 17 - The Laughing Room 22

Chapter 18 - The Saddest Eyes 23

Chapter 19 - Directions 25

Chapter 20 - Beauty and the Hustle 27

Chapter 21 - Kiss Me 30

Chapter 22 - The Day He Screamed 32

Chapter 23 - It's Your Fault 34

Chapter 24 - The Scream That Shook Walls 36

Chapter 25 - Night Walker 37

Chapter 26 - Hospitals.. 38

Chapter 27 - The Question That Broke Me 39

Chapter 28 - The Superpower Illusion 41

Chapter 29 - The God I Met in Madness 42

Chapter 30 - The Burning Bush 43

Chapter 31 - Underworld 44

Chapter 32 - 666 & The Circle 45

Chapter 33 - Silent Rain 46

Chapter 34 - Decoding Messages 47

Chapter 35 - The Awaken One 48

Chapter 36 - Shadowboxing & Target Practice 49

Chapter 37 - The Perfect Aim 50

Chapter 38 - Hoops and Guns 51

Chapter 39 - Telepathy & the Animal Army 52

Chapter 40 - Phones & Secret Agents 53

Chapter 41 - Undercover 54

Chapter 42 - Rooms & Doors 55

Chapter 43 - Maya and the Sisterhood 56

Chapter 44 - Witches 57

Chapter 45 - Violet the Psychic: Hospitalization #2 58

Chapter 46 - Tics and Talks (Hospitalization #2) 59

Chapter 47 - Elon Musk 61

Chapter 48 - Lil Wayne 62

Chapter 49 - H and Helicopters 63

Chapter 50 - UFO 64

Chapter 51 - Platform 93⁄4 65

Chapter 52 - Scrooge and the Third Eye 66

Chapter 53 - PBA 67

Chapter 54 - Dalai Fucking Lama 68

Chapter 55 - Pocahontas 69

Chapter 56 - Mrs. Daisy 70

Chapter 57 - Fountain of Youth 71

Chapter 58 - The Universe Speaking to Me: Hallucinations and the Hamptons
.... 73

Chapter 59 - Durga Goddess: Worshiping the Moon and the Sun 74

Chapter 60 - Mission: Africa 75

Chapter 61 - Rihanna the Oracle and the Hellsinger 77

Chapter 62 - Phoenix and the Universe 78

Chapter 63 - Rome Was Built in a Day 79

Chapter 64 - Ancient Gods and Jesus 80

Chapter 65 - Turning Water into Wine 81

Chapter 66 - Malice 82

Chapter 67 - The Judge's Words 83

Chapter 68 - The Pain That Broke the Spell 84

Chapter 69 - Severe Depression 85

Chapter 70 - When My Mind Betrayed My Heart 86

Chapter 71 - My Significant Other 88

Chapter 72 - The Seer 90

Chapter 73 - The End 92

Chapter 74 - Looking Back at Baby Jenn 93

Chapter 75 - The Party 94

Chapter 76 - Drugs 95

Chapter 77 - "The Dance and the Goodbye" 97

Chapter 78 - Psychosis 98

Chapter 79 - Psychosomatic Pain 99

Chapter 80 - When the Mind Makes Its Own Truth 100

Chapter 81 - What's Normal? 101

Chapter 82 - The Knowing 102

Chapter 83 - The Lightness 104

Chapter 84 – The Beginning 105

Chapter 85 - The Multiverse Inside Me 106

Chapter 86 - Bipolar Mukbang 108

Chapter 87 - A Letter From My Husband 109

Chapter 88 - One Piece 111

Acknowledgments 113

Final Reflection 114

Epilogue 116

Prologue: The Girl Who Danced with Demons

They said I was sick. That I had lost my mind. But I remember the wind dancing with me. I remember the way the rain paused the moment I did, as if the sky itself was listening. Before I was hospitalized, I was a woman in love with life. A mother. A wife. A dreamer. I worked hard, loved deeply, and held it all together. Until I couldn't. The world cracked open, and what poured through wasn't just pain, it was visions, symbols, frequencies, messages I thought were from God... or maybe the universe. Maybe both. In the psych ward, they called it delusion. But how could it be a delusion when birds flew in sync with my thoughts? When strangers whispered things that felt like prophecy? When the music on the radio echoed questions I hadn't even spoken aloud? I was grieving more than just my mind. I was grieving the loss of trust. The loss of control. The loss of my son's tiny hand in mine. And in that grief, something ancient woke inside me, a sleeping warrior goddess, opening her eyes.

This isn't just a story about psychosis. This is a story about awakening. About how pain can be sacred. How the mind can break open to let the spirit in. This is the story of how I danced like I was fighting demons... because maybe I was.

Chapter 1 - Grandiose, God, and I
The Purpose-Driven Delusion

About a month after I was released from the hospital, I stumbled on something that shook me: a TikTok video about "Crystal Children"-souls who incarnated to awaken the planet. They'd already lived through lifetimes of lessons, and now they were here as beacons.

The traits they listed? They felt... like me: Highly sensitive, even to light. An inner drive toward something bigger. My third eye had always felt open. I was never one to follow the crowd. An old soul. A radiant energy that made people spill their pain to me like I was their personal therapist. The wildest part? I was sober. No weed. No alcohol. Just me, Spirit, and whatever frequency had cracked me open. I'd used weed only to cope with physical pains during my battle with psychosis, a risky choice, but my tolerance was high. I messaged an old cop friend on Facebook, not to join the force, but because I genuinely thought I had something divine to offer.

Chasing purpose wasn't new. I'd been chasing it since I was seventeen, when I bought The Purpose Driven Life. I never finished it, but I passed it along to a Christian friend.

During that euphoric period, I truly believed I was chosen. The one. Like Neo in The Matrix. The Holy Grail in a world gone numb. I believed I could end the war. Bridge souls. Unite humanity. Maybe that is still my purpose. But then... came the crash. A manic episode. My body started rebelling, with seizures, stuttering, and temporary blindness. It felt like I was Scott Summers from X-Men, losing control of my power. Actually, no, I thought I was the "X" in X-Men. The missing link. The fine China soul too sacred to break. That's when Kina was born. She's me, but not. You'll meet her again and again. A character, a vision, a splinter of psychosis... or maybe something more.

Chapter 2 - The Universe Inside Me

Two years ago, I felt it. Not an idea, a summons. A soul-level call to write a story. A story about the Divine returning to Earth. I believed I was writing a prophecy disguised as fiction. And I believed that story would come true. What shook me was how much of it already had.

The visions I had showed up in real life, in headlines, in birds, in the shape of clouds. Fox News quoted scripture. Volcanoes erupted.

Artifacts of Jesus were found. It all aligned with my vision. And I thought: I am the chosen one. World peace. Heaven on Earth. I'm part of it. I thought I had Saturn's rings spinning inside me. That I was a portal. That the universe lived in my belly. It sounds crazy, I know. But was it? I believed I had divine pitch. That every step, every good deed, was a sacred test. Like I was walking in the footsteps of the ancestors. Even now, I still wonder...

Chapter 3 - The Day She Screamed

One night, I was holding my infant son. I had been sitting there for almost two hours. Cradling him softly, rocking him until my arms were tired, but my heart was full. I wanted him to feel safe. I wanted him to feel loved so deeply, quietly and completely. And then, out of nowhere… I saw her. A version of me screaming… not just yelling. Screaming in pain. Screaming at me. Her face was twisted in rage.

Her energy was violent. And I froze. I don't know what was happening. I was just holding my baby… and suddenly I was being confronted by a version of myself I didn't know existed. But I understand that the scream was never meant to hurt me. It was the wounded version of me…That never felt seen or soothed or safe. She had been buried for a long time. Ignored, pushed down and silenced. And in that still, quiet moment of love, she finally had a space to speak. That scream wasn't anger; it was grief and longing. It was a desperate cry to be loved the way I was loving my child. And I realized I was doing something generations before me couldn't do. I wasn't just putting my baby to sleep... I was holding my inner child at the same time. Healing is strange like that. It comes when you least expect it.

And sometimes it shows you the parts of yourself that were screaming to be heard all along.

Chapter 4 - The Poltergeist

Every night, I sat just inches from the television, cross-legged on the carpet, watching Nickelodeon's kids' shows. I was completely absorbed, especially at night, when the glow of the screen felt safer than the darkness behind me. Because in our house, we didn't just live with shadows. We lived with an evil spirit. It hurled dressers, tables, chairs, whatever it could grasp in its rage. It filled our home with screams that rattled the walls and burrowed into our bones. But the worst part wasn't that the spirit was invisible. The worst part was that it had a face. A man. That man was supposed to protect his wife and children. That man was my father.

I remember one night in particular: I was sitting crisscross in front of the TV, pretending the cartoons could drown out the chaos. Behind me, my sisters cried, shouting in panic as the screams from upstairs grew sharper, more terrifying. One of them grabbed the phone, desperate to reach our mother's older sister. I turned to her and said, calm and matter-of-fact: "Call the police. Auntie can't do anything for us. Just call the police." Then I turned back to the television, as if nothing had happened. Looking back now, I wonder: was I numb even then, or was I simply a cold child?

Chapter 5 - Hear No Evil, Say No Evil, See No Evil

There are sentences a child should never hear, words that should never exist inside a home, threats that should never reach the ears of a baby or a little girl who doesn't yet understand what danger is. But I grew up hearing them anyway, not because they were said to me, but because they were said around me, in the air I breathed, in the walls that shook during fights, in the silence that followed.

One of the things my mom told us years later, when we were finally old enough to understand, was that during one of their fights, my father once said to her: "I'll cut your nipples off and eat them like sashimi."

I remember sitting there in shock when she told us, not because I remembered the moment, I didn't, I was too little, too young, too unaware of what violent language even meant back then. But suddenly, so many things about my childhood made sense: the fear, the tension, the way my body reacted even when my mind didn't understand why, the freezing, the silence, the instinct to stay small and invisible.

I realized I didn't need to remember the details to know the truth; I grew up in a home where violence lived in the atmosphere.

Children don't need threats to be directed at them for those threats to wound them; hearing violence is its own kind of trauma. You don't need to understand a threat to feel it, you don't need to comprehend danger to sense it.

My trauma wasn't tied to a single moment; it was tied to an environment, a home where yelling was normal, where doors slammed, where my mother shrank in fear, and where violent language floated in the air like poison. We were too young to smell it. So, when I grew older, and my psychosis twisted old fears into new delusions, it wasn't pulling from a hidden memory; it was pulling from a violent childhood, from a nervous system shaped by chaos, from echoes of fights I was too young to decode. I didn't inherit a single moment of trauma; I inherited the atmosphere of it.

5

And now I understand something I couldn't understand then:

The violence wasn't aimed at my body, but it landed everywhere else; my sense of safety, my childhood, my nervous system, my understanding of love, my ability to trust peace. Sometimes the wound isn't what happened; sometimes the wound is what you heard.

.

Chapter 6 - The Chanting Sisters

I must have been about five years old. The room was crowded with toys and covered in colorful pictures, except for one wall. That wall wasn't a wall at all. It was a mirror, stretching wide and still, reflecting us back. My sisters sat on the floor, eating pizza and laughing. I stared into the glass and felt, somehow, that it wasn't just a mirror. I walked over to my older sister, who was seven then, and leaned close to her ear.

"They're watching us," I whispered.

"Let's sing a song about how we want to live with Mom." So together, our small voices rose in chant:

"We want Mom. We love Mom."

I can't explain how I knew, at five years old, that the mirror was a window, that someone was on the other side. I can't explain how I understood that this was no ordinary day, but the day that would decide where my sisters and I would live, and with whom.

Chapter 7 - Behave or Else

When I was four years old, I remember walking past my father one day while he was scolding my sister. He snapped at her in a tone that froze the air:

"You better behave, or you'll get a 똥꼬에 주사 맞는다 again." ("I'll give you a shot in your butt.")

The moment I heard those words, my entire body reacted: a full-body shiver, a fear I couldn't explain. I didn't understand why it scared me so much, only that it did. I kept walking, pretending I didn't hear it, but something inside me tightened. It felt like my body remembered something, even if my mind didn't. I never thought much about that moment growing up. I tucked it away the way children do, quietly, without understanding, without language for it.

Life moved on. But during psychosis, that old fear came back in a tidal wave. I was in the shower, on my knees, the water hitting my back while my thoughts spiraled faster than I could keep up. I became convinced the CIA and FBI were watching me through heat-motion sensors. I started signing frantically with my hands, crying, panicking, trying to communicate something I couldn't name.
And that childhood moment, that sentence, replayed in my mind like it was happening all over again.

In that state, my brain twisted that old fear into a new delusion: that maybe something terrible had happened to me when I was young, something I couldn't remember, something hidden in the cracks of my memory.

But here is the truth: I don't know what, if anything, happened back then. I don't have clear memories. I don't have facts. I don't have answers. All I had, both as a child and during psychosis, was fear.

Psychosis grabbed that fear, amplified it, distorted it, and convinced me it meant something bigger, darker, and heavier than I could understand. That's what psychosis does. It makes emotions feel like evidence. It turns fear into certainty. It fills in the blanks with nightmares.

8

Even now, I still don't know the truth of that moment from childhood. What I do know is this: The fear was real. The delusion was real. But the memory itself is unclear. My body remembered something my mind still can't fully name, and sometimes, that's the most honest answer I can give.

Chapter 8 - What the Mind Remembers

I was five the day they sat me on my mother's lap in a room that didn't feel meant for children. There were bars on the windows, uniforms everywhere, and a kind of silence that made you feel like you weren't supposed to speak. Someone slid a paper in front of me: a drawing of a little girl's body. My mother whispered, it's okay, even though nothing about it felt okay. They asked me to show where he touched us. I remember looking at the picture and feeling something heavy sit in my chest. Not fear of the man. Fear of getting him in trouble. Fear of telling the truth. So, I pointed close to the places he touched. Not exactly. Five-year-old survival doesn't always look like honesty. Sometimes it looks like protecting the person who hurt you because that's all you know.

After that day, the memory faded. Not gone... Just blurry, like a photograph left out in the sun. And then years later, during my psychosis, everything came back in the loudest, most terrifying way.

My mind cracked open old doors I thought were locked forever. I became convinced something even worse had happened to me, something I couldn't fully remember. Every time I thought about that man, the memory slipped away again, like my brain refused to give me the full picture. During my episode, I cried for days, certain I had been hurt in ways I couldn't name. Certain I was unsafe.

Certain my body remembered something my mind couldn't. I still don't know if what I felt was a delusion, a resurfaced trauma, or a memory my brain tried to erase to protect me.

What I do know is this:

The fear was real, the confusion was real, the panic was real and the child version of me lived through something she never should have. My body carried out the truth even when my mind couldn't find it. And that is something I'm still learning how to hold.

Chapter 9 - City Lights

I was too young when chaos started. Not the loud, obvious kind. The quiet kind, the kind where your stomach drops but you don't understand why yet. One night stood out for me. It was dark, very dark, but everything around us glowed. The city lights made the streets look like daytime dressed up in neon. People moved in waves along the sidewalks, a blur of legs and voices and bags swinging at their sides.

I remember thinking the world felt too big, too fast, too bright for how small we were. My sisters and I were with my dad, three little girls, ages three, five, and seven, shuffling into my mom's car as he dropped us off. My sisters climbed into the back seat. I sat in the front, feeling proud, like being five meant I was halfway to grown. We barely pulled out into traffic before my oldest sister started crying. Not the loud tantrum kind. The scared kind. My mom glanced into the rearview mirror. "What's wrong?" My sister pointed to the back seat, the place where my mom's purse should have been.

"He took it," she whispered.

My mom slammed on the brakes.

"What do you mean he took it? Who took it?" "Dad," my sister cried. "He took your purse."

The next moments blurred together like a movie missing frames. My mom pulled over, got out of the car, and I remember the slam of her door echoing too loud in my little chest. She started yelling at the night, at the stolen purse, at the life she was trapped in.

Then, suddenly, people were everywhere. They crowded around the car, staring, pointing, trying to figure out what was happening. My sisters cried harder in the backseat, tiny bodies shaking against their seatbelts. But I didn't cry. I just watched.

Five years old, sitting stiff and silent in the passenger seat while strangers surrounded us as if we were a spectacle. I remember lights flashing, police lights, street lights, headlights, all blending into one bright smear across the windshield. The cops came. My mom argued.

11

My sisters sobbed, and I sat there, absorbing everything like a sponge I didn't know I would carry into adulthood.

That is all I remember. A purse stolen. A car full of children. A mother pushed past her breaking point. A father disappearing into the night. And me, learning too early how to freeze when the world became too much. I didn't understand the weight of that night until years later. But somewhere in that chaos, in the yelling, the lights, the strangers pressing in, I think a small part of me cracked open. A part that learned that sometimes the people who are supposed to protect you are the ones who create the storm. And maybe that is why, years later, someone could look at me and say,

"You have the saddest eyes I've ever seen."

Because the sadness didn't start with adulthood. It didn't even start in that car. It began long before that, in a place I was too young to understand, a place my mind cannot fully remember but my body never forgot.

Chapter 10 - I Didn't Get Pancakes Either

I was maybe five or six. It was supposed to be pancake day. My best friend and I were so excited we skipped breakfast. But when we got to school... nothing. No pancakes. No syrup. Just disappointment.

My friend, the only Black kid in our class, asked the teacher for food. She got a bag of Goldfish. She looked at me kindly, like always, and offered me one. I shook my head. Then I got up and said: "I didn't eat either. I thought it was pancake day too." The teacher stared at me, dead-eyed. "You're lying," she said. "You saw her get snacks, now you want some too." I sat down. Stomach empty. Face burning. She didn't ask. She didn't care. We were the only Asian kids. My friend, the only Black girl. And in that moment, I learned what it meant to starve and be silenced at the same time.

Chapter 11 - The Devil All Around Us

I was in the fifth grade the day the world grew bigger, and darker, in my eyes. My parents were watching a Korean program called 119, our version of 911. I sat just inches from the TV, the glow washing over my face. On the screen, cops chased criminals through cramped streets, sirens echoing off buildings, everything moving fast and loud. At first, I watched it the way kids watch everything, curious, wide-eyed, waiting for it to make sense. Then I turned to my parents and asked: "Is this a movie?" They said, "No. It's real life." And instantly, hot tears rolled down my cheeks. I didn't fully understand why I was crying. I just knew something in me cracked open.

Because up until that moment, I thought evil belonged to America. I thought the world outside my home, especially the world my parents came from, was safer, softer, untouched by the kind of danger I'd already felt as a child. The truth is, I already knew what danger looked like. I knew it in the way my mother flinched. In the silence after shouting. In the heaviness of rooms where love and fear coexisted. That was personal danger. The kind you learn in whispers and footsteps and thick, unspoken tension. But 119 showed me something different. A new kind of danger. A danger that lived outside the walls of my childhood home. The danger of the world. Of strangers. Of violence that had nothing to do with my family. Danger with its own language, its own laws, its own shadows. And that realization was overwhelming. It wasn't just, "Bad things happen." I already knew that. It was, "Bad things happen everywhere." The world suddenly felt enormous, full of places I couldn't predict, people I couldn't read, situations I had no control over.

For a little girl who was already scared at home, realizing the outside world had its own darkness was too much. My tears weren't just confusion; they were grief. The kind of grief that comes from losing innocence twice: Once inside the house I grew up in, and again in front of a glowing TV screen showing me that danger wasn't just personal, it

14

was universal. That day taught me something I didn't have words for at the time: You can be unsafe in more than one language.

I learned, too early: There is danger in every language, in every country, in every story. The devil isn't in one place. He's woven through all of us. He's all around us.

Chapter 12 - I'm Not a Fighter

I was in the fifth grade the first time I snapped. One of the boys in my class said something about my mom, something nasty and sharp that sliced straight through me before I could even process the words. All I remember is the heat. One second, I was standing there, the next second I was on top of him, swinging. I jumped on him and punched him over and over with everything I had in my small fifth-grade body. Fists landing, breath shaking, his sister crying in the corner. The whole room went blurry around us. I don't remember what anyone else did. I don't remember a teacher's voice or a friend pulling me back. I just remember the rage. Pure, wild, animal rage. It wasn't about being tough. It wasn't about wanting to fight. It was about the one rule that lived deeper than language inside me: You don't talk about my mom.

I thought that would be it. A one-time explosion. But it wasn't. At Korean school on Saturdays, the place where we were supposed to learn hangul and culture and "proper behavior," the same boy tried me again. He said something else, something smart and cutting, and that switch inside me flipped just as fast. I jumped on him again.

Same story. Same fists. Same anger. Two different places, same boy, same outcome. Do I feel bad? No. Did he deserve it? Absolutely.

I'm not proud of the violence, but I'm not going to lie and pretend I regret defending the one person who held my world together. I'm not a fighter by nature. I hate yelling. I hate conflict. I shut down when people scream. But there have always been these moments in my life where something in me refuses to stay quiet. Where my body moves before my brain can catch up. Where the girl who usually freezes... doesn't. Back then, I didn't have words for it.

Now I know: Even if I'm not a fighter, I have always been someone who will go to war for the people I love.

Chapter 13 - The Devil Inside

When I was sixteen, I found myself at a church retreat in the Catskills. It was one of those early experiences where faith was still something new and a little fragile for me. I was a newcomer to

Christianity, and this was probably my first or second retreat ever. We spent the days doing all sorts of group activities, skits, plays, and bonding exercises that were meant to bring us closer together.

One afternoon, we were sitting in a circle, and someone asked the group a simple question: "Who do you want to be like when you grow up?" When it was my turn, I answered from the heart. I said, "I want to be like Jesus." It felt like the most natural thing to say. After all, isn't that what we were there to learn? But then a boy I thought was a friend looked straight at me and said, "You know who else wanted to be like Jesus? The devil."

In that moment, I felt a cold wave of confusion and hurt wash over me. I didn't know what to say. I was new to all of this, and here was someone twisting my earnest answer into something dark and unsettling. I felt like I had been judged for wanting something pure, and it made me second-guess myself. It made me feel small and silenced. Looking back now, I realize that was one of those moments that taught me how easily people can use faith to shame or confuse others. But it also taught me to hold onto my own truth. I wanted to be like Jesus because I wanted to be kind, not because I was trying to be perfect or powerful. And no one could take that intention away from me.

Chapter 14 -Beneath the Long Sleeves

When I was sixteen, I kept my pain hidden under long sleeves in the middle of summer. My mother didn't understand why I refused to take off my shirt in the heat. And the day she found out the truth is a day I'll never forget. When she rolled up my sleeves and saw the cuts on my arms, I saw a look in her eyes I hadn't seen before. It was sadness mixed with shock, maybe even guilt. She hadn't realized how hard her discipline had hit us, how deep it went. But in that moment, all of that fell away, and it was just a mother seeing her child's hidden pain. She took me to a psychiatrist after that. I remember the waiting room, cold, dim, not a place that felt meant for a teenager. It felt like a place for people who were lost, and I sat there feeling like I didn't belong. But I also saw other kids and teens around me, kids who clearly needed help, and I wondered if I was one of them.

When we finally saw the doctor, he looked at me and quickly said, "You're bipolar." My mom was offended. In our culture back then, mental health wasn't something you talked about. It felt like an insult, not a diagnosis. We walked out of that office confused and hurt, dismissing his words. We didn't believe it then. We didn't look back at it. It was a label that felt too heavy, too sudden, and too unreal.

And for years, we never spoke of it again. It wasn't a moment of understanding. It was a moment we buried, a truth we weren't ready to hold. It wasn't until years later, when I had my first full psychotic break in 2019 that those words came back to us. That was when we finally understood what that doctor had seen all along. It took time. It took more pain. It took a journey we never expected. But eventually, we came to see that what we dismissed was the truth we had to face. And that was the beginning of finally understanding what was really happening inside me.

Chapter 15 - The Tell in My Hands

There are moments in life that seem ordinary on the surface, just a family gathering, just a game around the table, but they reveal something deeper that you don't fully understand until later.

I remember one of those moments clearly. We were sitting around as a family, playing Texas Hold'em. My sister's boyfriend was there, everyone was laughing and having a good time, and I was holding a really good hand. I was proud of my poker face; my expression didn't give anything away. But there was one thing I couldn't hide: my hands. They were shaking uncontrollably, and I didn't even realize it until my mom noticed. It was like my body had its own tell that I wasn't aware of.

In that moment, my mom saw something I didn't. It was a little sign that maybe I was wired a bit differently, that my body sometimes spoke the anxiety or intensity I tried to keep hidden. It was just a small moment, a family card game, but it was one of those times that hinted at something deeper, a clue that maybe my emotions ran a little differently, even when I didn't realize it.

Chapter 16 - Pain Displacement

There was a time when I actually felt safe. It was right after we finally escaped the giant hell house and moved into our tiny two-bedroom apartment. I remember our first Christmas there so clearly. We went from having a huge tree overflowing with gifts to a tiny little potted plant with a red ribbon tied on top. That was our Christmas now small, quiet, simple. But for the first time, it felt peaceful. Instead of tearing open presents in a big house filled with noise and tension, we were all cuddled together in one queen-sized bed, and my mom sat at the edge holding our gifts in her lap. I will never forget it. She handed me a small stationary notebook, the kind from cute Korean stationery shops, and I remember feeling something I had not felt in years. Peace. A soft peace we never had before.

But peace rarely lasts in homes shaped by old wounds. My mom was working two jobs, raising three little girls entirely on her own, and she was barely ninety pounds, yet she carried the weight of a broken marriage and the pressure of survival on her back. Now that I look back, I can see how much she was drowning.

One day she came home and saw a Warheads candy wrapper on the table.

"Where did you get this?" she asked.

I told her I borrowed ten cents from our neighbor and bought it from the ice cream truck. All I remember after that is her closing the blinds, and then the discipline began.

In many Asian households, discipline is seen as normal. Getting hit is normal. Being whooped is normal. It is not viewed as abuse; it is viewed as culture and tradition a method of raising children passed down without question. But my mom did not know her own strength. She did not know softness because no one had ever been soft with her. The violence did not begin with us. It began with my father. The beatings he inflicted on her were so severe that the pain did not end with her it displaced itself onto us. She carried a pain tolerance nothing like ours.

20

What felt normal to her was far more than our small bodies could handle. She hit us harder than she realized, harder than she meant to, harder than any child should ever be hit.

And the truth is, I know she was not trying to hurt us. She was trying to raise us in the only language she had ever been taught. She did not swing with cruelty; she swung with all the pain she never healed.

This is what I call pain displacement. Hurt people rarely pass down wisdom... they pass down whatever was done to them. The discipline continued as we got older. One time in high school, I could not pull my skinny jeans up because there was a purple, swollen lump on my thigh the size of a football.

Even now, I do not blame her. I truly believe she did not know. She did not understand how hard she hit us. To her, it was normal. In her mind, Asians use hitting as discipline, and that is how she was raised, so that is what she repeated. It does not make it right, but it does make it understandable.

My mom did the best she could with the tools she had. She did not have therapy. She did not have support. She did not have rest, or a partner, or space to breathe. She had three little girls looking up at her, and every day felt like a war she had to fight alone. Her hands were not cruel, they were tired. Her voice was not hateful, it was overwhelmed. Her discipline was not meant to break us; it was the only way she knew how to keep us in line. And that is why this memory hurts and heals me at the same time. I can forgive her because I finally understand that none of it was ever truly her fault. She did not know where to put her pain, so it landed on us. Now I get to be the one who stops it.

Chapter 17 - The Laughing Room

The room was small, one of those generic doctor's office cubes with beige walls, faded anatomy posters, and that sterile paper that crackles like a threat when you move. I remember staring at the ceiling tiles. One of them was peeling at the corner, like it was trying to escape. I was there to explain something I didn't even understand: the seizures. The blackouts. The slipping. I spoke carefully, like I was holding glass in my mouth. Vulnerable. Raw. Still clinging to the hope that someone, anyone, might take me seriously. At first, the doctor nodded as if he was listening. Until he wasn't. He leaned back in his chair, smirked, and said: "Next time you have a seizure, tell your friend to kick back, grab a beer, and record it." Time stopped.

My breath caught. My face burned. My hands curled into themselves, silent fists of shame. He then showed me a video of a woman having a seizure and said, "Anything triggers this lady. Just watch." It was hard to watch someone go through what I experienced, while the doctor treated it like a spectacle. Looking back, I should have replied: "Is what you're showing me even legal? Isn't this violating other people's rights?" That being said, I never went back.

Chapter 18 - The Saddest Eyes

I didn't realize how many warnings life tried to give me back then. They didn't look like dramatic revelations or booming signs from the sky. They looked like small, uncomfortable moments I shrugged off because I didn't know how to trust myself yet.

One of those moments came wrapped in the kind of late-night weirdness I used to mistake for "normal." It started with my wallet. I didn't even know it was missing until my ex told me his mom had found it in the backseat of his car. And instead of calling him, or waiting to see me in person, she solved the mystery in the most unhinged way possible, by calling my dentist office and asking for my phone number. And the part that still blows my mind? They gave it to her. To this day, I don't know who at that front desk answered the phone or why they didn't stop for even a second before handing out my personal information like a free sample at Costco. But in that moment, it didn't even register to me how much of a violation that was. Back then, I had been trained to normalize chaos.

Later that night, she showed up to return it. It was dark outside, the kind of quiet suburban darkness that feels too still, too staged. She stepped out of her car wearing all black, like she had just come from a funeral or a church service. A silver cross necklace dangled over her chest, catching the porch light every time she moved. She looked…holy. Or at least, she wanted to. But I knew better. She didn't believe in God. She believed in image.

She held out my wallet like it was something sacred she had rescued, not something she discovered after snooping and dialing every office with my name on file. And as she studied me, her eyes narrowed into this dramatic, probing squint, like she wanted to read every secret I had ever tried to hide. Then she said it. "You have the saddest eyes I've ever seen." For a second, it felt like time froze. Not because the words were wise or spiritual, but because of how heavy they landed on my chest. I didn't know what to say back. She wasn't someone I trusted enough to be vulnerable with, but she also wasn't wrong.

Something inside me was already unraveling, long before I understood the words bipolar or psychosis or episode. She saw it before I did, even if she didn't understand what she was looking at. Or maybe she just liked being the kind of person who dropped dramatic lines in the dark. Either way, that night stayed with me. Not because of the wallet or the ridiculous detective act she pulled to get my number. Not even because of the cross necklace she wore like a costume. It stayed because, for the first time, someone said out loud what I didn't have the courage to admit: I was hurting, and it showed. Back then, I didn't leave even when life whispered, You don't belong here anymore. I wasn't ready. But looking back now, that night feels like the universe tapping me on the shoulder, and me pretending not to feel it.

Chapter 19 - Directions

There are certain stories from our lives that don't seem important when they're happening. They feel small, simple, just another moment in the blur of growing up and becoming who we are. It's only later, when we walk back through them, that we realize how much they say about us, about the people around us, and about the ways we've learned to protect our own peace.

One of those stories happened about ten years ago, back when GPS was more "good luck" than guidance, and I was as directionally lost as a person could be. Tell me a street name and I'd still need someone to physically point in the direction of "that way." So when my maid of honor planned a bridal shower for me in the city, I was excited, grateful, and quietly panicked about how I would get home. The party itself was perfect. My sisters, my cousin, my friend, everyone laughing, celebrating, taking pictures in our little hotel room like everything was exactly as it should be.

But as the night faded into early morning and people started drifting out, my maid of honor said the words that tightened something inside me: "I have to leave at 6 a.m., so you'll have to get home on your own."

For most people, that might not sound like a big deal. But for me? Navigating the city alone felt impossible, morning, night, didn't matter. I knew I'd get lost. I knew I'd panic. And I knew I'd end up calling someone, crying from a random block I couldn't pronounce. I tried to find a solution. I asked my cousin to stay with me, to sleep at the hotel, so I wouldn't have to figure it out alone, but she had church that morning.

My sisters were heading home too. So I made the only choice that felt safe, I went with my family. I wasn't abandoning anyone. I wasn't being dramatic. I was just trying not to get lost, not physically, not emotionally. But my maid of honor didn't see it that way. She got upset. Then really upset. And then she wrote a full letter to my husband, accusing me of abandoning her. I remember reading it and thinking, all this… because I didn't want to get lost in the city?

In the end, she backed out of the wedding. And I walked away from the whole thing with something unexpected: a story that says so much about who I was back then, a girl who cared too much about disappointing people and not enough about her own limits. Walking down memory lane isn't always sweet. Sometimes it's messy, confusing, unfair. But looking back, I see the truth I couldn't see then: I wasn't wrong. I just needed someone who understood me. And she wasn't it.

Chapter 20 - Beauty and the Hustle

No matter where I worked, I always ended up becoming the head bartender. Not because I asked, not because I pushed, but because I was good. Fast. Outgoing. Sharp. A natural. I could make a cocktail look like a magic trick, flip between guests like I had wings, and still sell more than every bartender standing next to me. My sales were never just higher, they were doubled. Triple. At one club, my numbers hit $3,000 while the others barely rang at $1,000. It wasn't bragging. It was the truth. I hustled. I showed up. I earned it. So, when I started at a craft cocktail lounge in Queens and once again became the head bartender, it felt normal, almost expected. People used to watch me work like they were watching a tennis match. Their heads would follow me left to right, right to left, as if the whole bar was the court and I was the ball. I had rhythm. I had presence. I had skill. And everyone knew it. Everyone except the owner.

One night, while we were closing out and counting our drawers, my manager, who had never worked a real shift in her life, pulled me aside. She said it straight-faced, like she was reading a grocery list. "The boss thinks you're stealing." I remember staring at her, confused, shocked, almost insulted by how casually she dropped something so heavy. The girls around me just shrugged, pretending not to know anything, pretending not to hear. I learned later they knew exactly what was happening, and they let it. She told me the owner had been watching me on the cameras all day, opening the POS system from his tablet, tracking my movement like I was a criminal instead of the bartender keeping his business alive.

I went home that night hurt, anxious, heart pounding. And instead of sleeping, I sat up writing an email: "Just letting you know, he paid this way. She paid for him. They split the bill.

This guest tipped cash…"

I remembered every transaction. Every detail. Every seat. Every drink. That's the kind of worker I was.

The next day, after checking all the cameras, he finally admitted: "You're right." But no apology. No "I'm sorry I accused you." No "I should've trusted you." Not even a hint of respect. Just a cold confirmation that he was wrong, and that was somehow enough for him. For most people, maybe that would've been fine.

But for me? For someone who gave everything, my speed, my heart, my hustle? It felt like a slap in the face. I remember thinking, If you can accuse me so easily, you don't deserve me when I work this hard. So I handed in my two weeks and walked away. Not out of weakness, out of dignity.

Years later, I was working as the head bartender in a steakhouse when one of my old regulars from that cocktail bar walked in. We laughed, caught up, reminisced about those busy nights. And then, in the middle of our conversation, he said something that made the floor drop under me. "You know why you got fired, right?" I blinked. "I didn't get fired. I quit." He looked at me, sympathetic. "No… the girls tried to get you fired. They told the owner you were stealing. They made up stories. They wanted you gone." I stood there speechless. My mind didn't race, it shattered. Because suddenly it made sense. The looks. The shrugs. The silence that night. The owner's accusations. The way no one stood up for me.

It wasn't him who doubted me. It was them. The ones who watched me hustle circles around them. The ones who couldn't match my speed, my energy, my numbers. The ones who envied me enough to lie. And that regular? He didn't lie. He was part of their circle. He heard it firsthand. I remember standing there behind the bar, holding a drink in my hand, smiling through the crack in my chest.

Because that's what I did back then, I held myself together in public while breaking in private. Beauty and the hustle. That was me. I could make a perfect cocktail with steady hands, even on the days my heart was shaking. I learned that no matter how good you are, someone will always try to dim your light. But I also learned something else: They didn't take my shine. They exposed theirs. And I kept going. Stronger.

Smarter. And with a work ethic no lie could ever erase.

Chapter 21 - Kiss Me

There was a restaurant I worked at, same grind, same rhythm, same story. Me behind the bar, slinging cocktails for a dinner shift packed with three hundred people. Most people drown in that kind of chaos. I thrived in it. The stack of tickets would pile so high it looked like a tower, and I'd move through it without missing a beat. Speed was my language. Efficiency was my comfort zone. Hospitality was my art. But the managers… they were the problem. The head manager was the type of man who needed control like oxygen, the type who puffed his chest out near the owners, the type who wanted everyone to think he ran the place, the type who once pulled out his own ID to show the cops because the owners couldn't find theirs, as if he owned the building, the street, the whole damn city. He hated when anyone shined brighter than him. And I did, every shift. He'd yell at me for talking to the owner, not because I did anything wrong, but because he couldn't stand being overshadowed by someone younger, faster, and better. And then there was the other one; the creepy short manager; his best friend; bad energy in a smaller package. Every night he'd tell me, "You have to come say bye to me before you go."

To anyone else, that might sound off. But to me, raised in Korean culture, where hierarchy is everything, it sounded normal. You say goodbye to the boss, you bow, you show respect. So, every night, before heading out, I'd run over and say, "I'm leaving now.

Goodnight." And then it turned weird. He'd lean in and say, "You didn't give me a kiss." At first, I brushed it off, laughed awkwardly, said no. But every night, he asked again. "Come on. Just a kiss."

Every. Single. Night. Then one evening he came up to me, eyes glowing like he was proud of something. "I told my wife about you," he said. "She said it's okay." I froze. "What? Told her what?" He smirked. "You know…" And that was it. Every instinct in my body screamed; every red flag lit up like a fire. Later, an old coworker messaged me and told me what I already suspected; he had been going around kissing the young hosts, cornering them, taking advantage. That flipped something inside me; the big-sister instinct, the protector, the part of me that refuses to let girls get hurt because I stayed silent. So, I texted the boss, the real boss, not the wannabe one. I told him what happened; everything. Not dramatic, not emotional, just the truth. After our messages… they didn't resign, they didn't leave quietly, they were fired. Both of them. The head manager and the creepy one. The duo. Gone. Because people like that never leave on their own; they get removed when someone finally speaks up. And for once, it wasn't the girl shrinking in fear, it wasn't the girl staying quiet, it wasn't the girl being pushed out. It was me, standing tall; me, telling the truth; me, protecting the ones after me. People always saw the beauty, people always saw the hustle, they rarely saw the spine. But it's always been there.

Chapter 22 - The Day He Screamed

There was a day I will never forget, not because something dramatic happened, but because something inside me changed. We drove home from the city. My husband was behind the wheel, focused on traffic. I sat in the passenger seat. His best friend, the one he's known since childhood, sat behind us in the middle. Next to him was his girlfriend, and beside her was a colleague they both worked with. Somehow the topic of room salons came up. It was casual at first, just guy talk, just conversation, until it wasn't. The colleague said quietly, almost shyly, "I don't go to those places... I feel bad for the women." And before the words finished leaving his mouth, my husband's best friend laughed. Laughed loud. Called him a wuss.

Told him to stop the bullshit. Mocked him like compassion was a weakness. It went on for five long minutes. Five minutes of bullying dressed up as "joking." Five minutes where the friend tried to crush any softness out of the colleague. Five minutes when everyone else stayed silent. And I couldn't take it anymore. I spoke up. Not for myself, but for the colleague; for the women who work in those places; for anyone who's ever been judged for choosing kindness. The colleague got dropped off, and that should have been the end of it. But instead... it escalated. Now the friend turned his energy on me. Suddenly his voice changed, stern, sharp, angry.

He leaned forward between the seats, yelling as if I had personally attacked him, like defending a stranger's dignity was a crime, like my voice somehow threatened his manhood. I kept calm. I told him, gently, repeatedly, "Just talk. Just calm down. There's no need to yell." But he didn't calm down. He got louder. His body lunged forward as far as the seatbelt allowed, his anger filling the entire car, his voice ricocheting off the windows like we were trapped inside a box. I remember looking straight ahead, feeling the sound of him rather than the words; feeling the way his presence swallowed the air; feeling the way my hands shook even though I tried to keep my face still. And what hurt the most? His girlfriend sat beside him, quiet, relaxed, watching the show as if this was entertainment. Her silence was louder than his screaming. Not a "stop," not a "calm down," not even a hand on his arm, just nothing.

A few days later, I confronted my husband. Not because he agreed with his friend, he didn't. Not because he wanted me hurt, he didn't. But because he didn't stop him. He was driving through heavy traffic, eyes on the road, mind on safety, and I don't blame him for that. But I needed to tell him how it felt to be a 120-pound woman, trapped in a moving car, with a six-foot man, leaning forward and screaming at me like I had offended the world. My body remembered. My mind remembered. I told him, "I will never let that man near my peace again." And I meant it. Sorry or not, excuses or not, childhood friend or not, my nervous system does not forget the feeling of being cornered, with no way out, while another woman sits silently beside him, choosing comfort over courage. That day didn't just show me who he was. It showed me who I would never allow in my life again.

Chapter 23 It's Your Fault

There was a newly opened restaurant I worked at, brand new staff, brand-new menus, and that fake honeymoon energy where everyone pretends the industry isn't the industry. I was managing at the time, juggling schedules, dealing with prep lists, putting out fires before the place even opened its doors. That's when I met him. Not a man, just a guy. Industry-adjacent. He worked behind the scenes in an office, the type who never gets his hands dirty but knows everything about everyone else's job. At first, it felt nice to talk to someone who understood hospitality from the inside.

We'd chat casually when he stopped by, nothing deep, nothing personal. Then one day, the topic of sexual harassment in hospitality came up. He brought it up. He laughed. And then he said, "You're in this industry. It's just part of the world, hun."I stared at him. "What does that mean?" He shrugged like it was obvious. "I mean… girls in this industry know what they're getting into. If you walk into this world, you should expect that kind of stuff. Women today complain too much." My face went cold. He kept going, blaming us, women, for the behavior of men; as if harassment was a "condition of employment," as if survival was a woman's responsibility, as if men couldn't be held accountable for anything. And all I could think was, If this is what he says out loud… I can't imagine what's said or done behind closed doors; what they say when no women are around; what they allow; what they normalize; what they excuse; what they laugh about; what they encourage. That thought made something inside me collapse… and then immediately rebuild itself stronger.

Because at that moment, I realized two things: First, men like him are the reason harassment is still alive in the industry; not the drunk customers; not the creepy managers; but the silent enablers who treat abuse like background noise. Second, I didn't want to be silent anymore. The disappointment hit me first, a heavy drop in my chest, like I lost a tiny piece of hope I didn't even know I was holding. But then the fire came, a fire that said, no more. Not for me. Not for the younger girls starting out. Not for anyone who shows up to do their job and ends up fighting battles no one sees. I didn't argue with him; he wasn't someone who deserved my breath. But I walked away knowing this: I will never let men like him decide what women should accept; not in hospitality; not anywhere; not ever. His ignorance didn't silence me, it awakened me.

Chapter 24 - The Scream That Shook Walls

I was downstairs in the bar's basement, humming to myself, just gathering inventory like I was grocery shopping in the dark. It was just another shift opening, just another quiet moment before the bar filled up. I headed back up the stairs, still humming, my mind on a hundred other things. Then, out of nowhere, my manager softly said my name, "Jenn." That's all it took. One gentle word.

I screamed as if I was being attacked, a full, raw, body-shaking scream that echoed off the basement walls. My body folded into a fetal position right there on the steps. And for a moment, everything went black, not like closing my eyes, but like I was suddenly outside myself, seeing that darkness all around me. I was watching myself curled up on the staircase from a place that felt like the edge of reality.

When I finally snapped back, my manager was staring at me, wide-eyed, asking if I was okay. Someone else came running, thinking something terrible had happened. And there I was, shaking it off, pretending I was fine, but knowing deep down that my body had just taken me somewhere else.

Chapter 25 - Night Walker

Sleepless nights were nothing new to me. For years, I lived in a rhythm where the sun went down, and my mind lit up. When I was younger, I'd stay awake for days at a time, slipping into the world of *World of Warcraft*, building characters with powers and skills I wished I had in real life. Gaming wasn't just a hobby, it was an escape, a place where being awake at 3 a.m. didn't feel strange. It felt natural. Safe. Almost purposeful. Even before that, as a kid, I could never fall asleep like everyone else. I'd lie awake for hours, never bored, just... awake. My body refused to rest like it belonged to another realm.

In high school, when the depression hit, I started keeping a bottle of NyQuil by my bed. I'd down the cap, desperate for silence in my head, only to wake up four hours later, wide-eyed, alert, as if the medicine never touched me. It was like my body didn't want sleep. Like it rejected it. Everything changed when I turned twenty-eight. I started bartending while going to school, and for the first time, my odd schedule made sense. Nights became my world. The rush of tickets, the glow of the bar lights, the laughter, the clinking of glasses, people were happiest at night, and I got to be part of that. I loved it.

Hospitality came naturally to me. I was good at it. But then my mental health caught up to me. COVID didn't help either, restaurants froze, cities shut down, and the life I built in the night crumbled overnight. The career I loved, the rhythm that finally made sense, slipped out of my hands. And then, after I finally recovered and started taking antipsychotics, my sleep flipped completely. Now I fall asleep anywhere between 6 p.m. and 10 p.m., and I wake up every morning between 3:00 and 4:30. It sounds odd to most people, but it works for me. I take naps when my son's at school, and honestly... I like this version of my life. I like the quiet mornings. I like that my body finally lets me rest, even if it's on its own strange terms. I used to walk through the night because I couldn't sleep. Now I walk through the morning because I finally can.

Chapter 26 - Hospitals

In 2019, something strange began happening to my body. My speech would suddenly slur. Sometimes, I couldn't speak at all. When I tried, the sound that came out was like a whale caught in its final breath. It didn't just happen once. Three times: 2019, then twice in 2021. Each time, I would lose consciousness. My body would give out. Once, I even lost control of my bowels. The first time, my husband rushed me to three hospitals in one night. At the last one, the doctor looked at me, half-listened, and suggested psychiatric admission. That's how I ended up at Flushing Hospital. I stayed ten days. They diagnosed me with bipolar disorder. To this day, I still don't understand how slurred speech and twitching became that diagnosis. I've always been emotionally stable. Before I had a child, I was a bartender. A damn good one. I worked at Nobu. I even started my own consulting company and met with a famous CFO from Korea. I walked into that meeting confident, prepared, and walked out with an $8,000 contract offer. But I turned it down.

Because I knew they planned to take my recipes and spread them across Asia without giving me royalties. I asked, they said no, so I walked away. That's who I was. I smiled all the time. Talked to everyone. I loved people. But after the last episode, the one where I believed I was a divine entity, everything changed. The third time, I needed hospitalization again. This time, a full psychiatric ward. Yes, I truly believed I was "the one." But even then, no one addressed the seizures. No one explored physical causes. It felt like the moment I was labeled mentally ill, everything else vanished. Maybe I was.

Maybe believing I was an angel sent from the Heavens. But I was also a woman whose body was failing. And no one seemed to be listening.

Chapter 27 - The Question That Broke Me

During my manic state, my husband took me to a sleep specialist, hoping someone, anyone, could explain what was happening to me. I wasn't sleeping. My body wouldn't rest. My mind felt electrified, buzzing, impossible to quiet. To stay awake and "focused," I listened to music constantly, rocking back and forth to the beat.

(And honestly, there's nothing calming about rocking back and forth; but at the time, it felt like the only thing keeping me grounded.)

We walked into the doctor's office, and I remember feeling wired, alert, and exhausted all at once. My husband tried to explain what had been going on, the sleeplessness, the racing thoughts, the erratic moods, and I tried my best to sit still.

Then the doctor turned to me and asked a question I never expected; a question that didn't just miss the mark, it cut straight through me.

"How do you know you were raped?" I froze. The world stopped. My breath disappeared into my chest. I stared at him, stunned, and the only thing that came out of my mouth was, "MY SISTERS." Then I stood up. And I walked out. Angry, betrayed, sick to my stomach. How could a doctor, someone trained to understand trauma, someone who should know the weight of that word, ask a question like that? How could he put doubt where there was already so much pain? How could he look at me, manic and terrified, and throw a grenade like that into the room?

In that moment, I didn't just cry for myself; I cried for every survivor who was ever questioned, every person who was ever doubted, every child who told the truth and was asked for proof. I thought I was there to get help. Instead, I walked out feeling the oldest hurt all over again. That day taught me something I'll never forget: Some wounds don't come from trauma itself; they come from the way the world responds to it.

For the record, I was never raped. But in my state of psychosis, I truly believed I was. I felt it in my bones, and the delusion held on tightly, convincing me the fear was real. And when that doctor asked his question, so casually, so carelessly, it wasn't curiosity, it was a wound.

A reopening of every fear I had ever carried. An echo of every survivor whose truth had been doubted. His insensitivity didn't reveal a memory; it revealed a truth I had never spoken out loud: that delusion can feel like memory, and doubt can cut just as deep as the trauma it implies. That question didn't just hurt. It broke something open inside me, a mix of anger, grief, and compassion for every person who was ever asked to prove their pain.

Chapter 28 - The Superpower Illusion

During my psychosis, I genuinely believed I had superpowers. Not in the cartoon way. In a way that felt spiritual. Ancient. Terrifying. Real. I thought I could see people's souls, their past lives, their sins, their pain, just by looking into their eyes. Sometimes, I believed I could enter someone's mind and heal their trauma just by being near them. I thought I absorbed pain and converted it into light.

There were moments I believed I was a reincarnated prophet. Other times, I thought I was watching alternate versions of myself, parallel timelines, trying to converge in one body. It sounds wild. And maybe it is. But back then, it wasn't a belief. It was an experience. Every vision. Every whisper. Every moment of clarity or collapse felt like truth. Like the veil had been lifted, and I could finally see the world as it really was. And the strangest part? Looking back... some of it doesn't feel entirely wrong. There was something sacred beneath the madness. A symbolic truth trying to break through the static. Maybe I wasn't a superhero. But I was someone shattered open so completely that I could see reality from a thousand broken angles. And in those fractures, I found something that looked like power.

Chapter 29 - The God I Met in Madness

I used to dream about writing a story about the divine. I thought it would be poetic: miracles, angels, a glowing light at the end of the tunnel. But when I actually met the divine, it didn't look like that. It looked like a locked psych ward. Court-ordered meds I didn't want.

Being separated from my son and wondering if I'd ever feel whole again. My body was tired. My mind didn't feel like mine. And still, something sacred was there. Not in thunder. Not in scripture. Not in a voice from the clouds. It was a kind nurse who called me "sweetheart" when I forgot how to speak. It was in the moment I chose to hold on, when everything inside me wanted to disappear. It was in my son's face appearing in dreams, reminding me why I couldn't give up.

Maybe the divine isn't a rescue. Maybe it's a presence. Something that stays with you, even in the dark. I still don't know exactly what I believe. I've gone from thinking I was chosen... to believing in nothing... to somewhere in between. But I know this: I've seen things that can't be explained. I've survived things most people don't come back from. And yes, I still want to write a story about the divine. But now I understand something I didn't before: This is it. Messy. Human. Shattered. Still sacred.

Chapter 30 - The Burning Bush

I don't remember exactly when it happened. Maybe it was night. Maybe the day had collapsed into itself like my sanity. But I remember the fire. Not physical fire, but a bush, blazing, raging, eternal. It was in front of me, behind my eyelids, in my chest. They would call it hallucination. But it didn't feel like madness. It felt like a message. Something, someone, was trying to speak through me.

Then my eyes rolled back. I started typing. Not with thought. Not with intention. My hands just moved, like they remembered something I hadn't learned yet. I was writing the Ten Commandments. But not those ones. These were mine. For the misfits. The seers. The wounded prophets. For the ones like me, who had died in their minds and come back with vision. That burning bush wasn't sent to scare me. It came to show me what I was becoming. Not a saint. Not a prophet. But something just as terrifying, a woman who remembered herself.

Chapter 31 - Underworld

My second hospitalization, in November 2021, was different. It felt more spiritual than clinical. I was unraveling, yes, but also awakening. Amid the chaos, I found something holy: connection, beauty, souls. But I also saw suffering, people walking the halls like ghosts, half-alive. There was one girl I'll never forget. Twenty-two. A mother. Lost. She didn't know how to shower anymore. Spoke like a child. All day she picked at her skin until it bled. When I asked her about high school, she froze, like I'd touched a wound no one could see. She was in the underworld. And something in me stirred. I believed I could bring people like her back to life, with kindness, patience, and presence. I saw myself as a monk. A healer. Here to guide the broken back to the sacred.

Chapter 32 - 666 & The Circle

In the ward, I noticed some people fixated on things, men, women, objects, and even numbers. The number 666 came up a lot. I didn't understand why people feared it. I didn't see it as evil. I saw it as geometry. I sat at a round table, marker in hand, paper before me, and began writing: 6... 6. 6. And then I saw a pattern. To me, a healthy mind was a perfect circle, whole, intact. But when that mind begins to spiral, it becomes. a six. Imbalance. Collapse. Distortion.

The number 6, repeated, 666, wasn't demonic. It was a signal. A frequency. A warning that something inside was off. I believed my circle was still whole. That it connected me to the Earth, to Spirit, to something bigger than myself. When you scribble sixes over and over, they naturally form a spiral. So when someone's inner circle is unbalanced, their circle doesn't remain clean, it spirals.

Chapter 33 - Silent Rain

One night, amid the chaos of seizure-like episodes, my eyes hurting so much I thought I was going blind, my hearing failing me in unpredictable waves, I stepped outside. It began to rain. But it wasn't hitting me. I could see it falling all around, lit by streetlight, shimmering, but not a single drop touched my skin. I looked up at the sky. Still, nothing. I was dry. Cloaked. Protected. In that moment, I was certain: I was something different.

Chapter 34 - Decoding Messages

There was a time I believed the CIA was watching me. Not out of fear, but out of purpose. I thought checks and notes held secret codes. That a hand-written dollar amount on a paycheck was a symbol. I tried calling cryptic numbers I believed were "activation lines." No one answered. Still, I kept dialing. After my second hospitalization, someone tried to deliver me a letter. I thought it was my acceptance. Like Hogwarts. But for the Awakened.

Chapter 35 - The Awaken One

Once, during a manic episode, I got a DM on Instagram from someone called The Awaken One or something like that. He told me I was chosen. A prophet. A leader of awakened minds. Months later, he turned out to be a scammer asking for charity donations. But in that moment? He felt like destiny.

Chapter 36 - Shadowboxing & Target Practice

At the third hospital, I spent hours shadowboxing in the hallway. I imagined I was fighting off demons, defending an entire town with my bare hands. I finger-shot door numbers like a sniper. Danced like I was training for war. They thought I was manic. Maybe I was. But to me, it was survival. Once the meds kicked in, that fire died. The fight left my body. And that scared me more than anything.

Chapter 37 - The Perfect Aim

Between my last two hospitalizations, I used to "practice" in the courtyard. I'd pretend to shoot leaves, lights, tires. I'd say I was playing "that duck shooting game." But really? I was Lara Croft. Spirit fingers. Divine vision.

Chapter 38 - Hoops and Guns

I was standing outside my courtyard when I noticed a basketball game across the street at a school. I told my husband I had to go, he looked confused. I couldn't explain; I just knew I had a job to do, even if I didn't yet know what that job was. I promised I'd be back when it was done. I walked over to the game. Around fifty men were there, some practicing, and some chatting on the sidelines. They let me step onto the court. I told myself I could make any shot I wanted.

Later, I overheard two men saying, "We could use her."

My heart leaped. This was my moment. I stepped to the center of the court. "I have perfect aim," I said.

"I can shoot guns with my eyes closed." Then I added,

"I can hit every ceiling light with my eyes closed." Using my fingers, I mimed shooting at the lights, one by one, feeling a rush of power.

When I was escorted out, I tried to go back in. I turned to one of the men and said: "Tell your boss. I'm here. I'm ready. I'm what everyone's been waiting for. You see, I'm the Virgin Mary... only I'm here with a vengeance. Call me Bloody Mary."

Chapter 39 - Telepathy & the Animal Army

I believed I could speak with animals. Squirrels. Dogs. Birds. They were my allies, helping me track evil, find predators, and protect the weak. I believed I was the Einstein of the divine world, decoding pain, and unlocking truth.

Chapter 40 - Phones & Secret Agents

Every time the hospital phone rang, I thought it was for me. That the CIA was calling, using fake names, like Valeria or Anton. One day, I picked up the phone and said: "I'm the one you're looking for. I'm her." Because in that moment? I was.

Chapter 41 - Undercover

After a tattoo consultation in Flushing, I walked home in the dark. Stick in hand. Half- blind. Shadow-fighting trees. I believed I was being watched, assessed, by the police. To see if I was worthy of a mission. And I was ready. I was the mission. My goal was to get people to believe this was heaven, the world we were standing on, but us humans were the ones turning it into Hell.

Chapter 42 - Rooms & Doors

During my third stay, I was moved into a new room. It once belonged to a girl I believed was an angel. A warrior. A soul surrounded by death. There was a rotating bookshelf near the bathroom. One book was about witches, a village, a tree, a woman with her arms outstretched in the sky. I thought it was me. My story. Every book I found seemed to confirm it. One was about a cop who was also an oracle. Another? About balance, magic, healing. Was it a coincidence? Or a message?

Chapter 43 - Maya and the Sisterhood

There was a girl in her twenties named Maya. On the day she arrived, she wore a shirt that said UMBRELLA ENT. She told me it stood for a group of underground rappers, her friends were part of it. But it reminded me of The Umbrella Academy, and I loved that idea, a group of gifted misfits changing the world from the shadows. One evening, I saw her brother visiting, Bible in one hand, and the other gently resting on her head. A deeply spiritual family. I even met her mom, cool, warm, and grounded. One night, we were all gathered by the window, coloring and drawing like little kids, passing time the only way we knew how. I laid out blankets on the floor like we were on a beach, creating a little escape. A girl named Sammy walked by, and I invited her to join. Maya wasn't thrilled, they'd almost gotten into a fight when Sammy was first admitted. Sammy was different too. She talked to spirits or at least claimed to. She mumbled often, spoke in riddles. That night, she told me about the Akashic Records, how the Egyptians believed it held the history of every soul. She also mentioned something called Hellsingers. I felt like maybe, just maybe, I could open up to her. But just as I was about to, Maya interrupted. She showed me a page she had colored: a Medusa skull, snakes coiled and alive with hot neon ink. I remember the intensity, how loud the colors felt. Later that night, she left that drawing behind. Next to it, a handwritten note: "Don't say anything or you'll regret it." I thought it was meant for me. I thought they were all watching, testing me, and waiting to see if I'd reveal my gifts to another agent in disguise.

Chapter 44 - Witches

I thought the beautifully gifted group of people I met at the hospital were witches, not the storybook kind, but real ones. Women with intuition, power, pain, and light. I believed we had all been chosen, accepted into some secret program of healing and awakening. One girl even wore a hoodie that said Salem Witch, and of course, I took it as a sign. Confirmation that I was right where I was meant to be.

Chapter 45 - Violet the Psychic: Hospitalization #2

There was this beautiful Russian woman named Violet. She was about my age, maybe a few years younger. She had two kids, a boyfriend she adored, and a free- spirited energy that stood out in a place like that. She was kind, radiant, and generous. I'll never forget when she gave away her Cartier bracelet, just handed it to another patient without hesitation. That's how we were in that hospital: stripped down, but strangely full of love. We shared everything we had, stories, snacks, and silence. I entered that place with a purpose: to share my story, to help the patients, and maybe even the field of psychology itself. I thought if they just knew everything that had happened to me, they'd understand something deeper.

When I first met Violet, she often had her eyes closed. She spoke with a soft, slurred voice, maybe from medication, maybe from exhaustion. But no matter how she moved or spoke, she swayed with the energy in the room like wind moved through her. She was like me. She had physical symptoms no one could explain: body tremors, seizures, and slurred speech, all dismissed as psychiatric.

Then one day, Violet confidently declared, "I'm psychic."

I rushed to her, almost in fear, worried that if she said it too loudly, they'd label her delusional.

But she looked at me, steady and calm, and said, "No, I told them already. They know."

She told us how she used to do readings for her coworkers, and how everything she predicted came true. I asked about the medications they had her on, hoping for some kind of answer. But none of them addressed what we were both feeling physically. They only treated the psychiatric. Neither of us seemed like textbook cases. Not until we started saying the things they didn't understand.

Chapter 46 - Tics and Talks (Hospitalization #2)

On the second-to-last night of my stay at a hospital in Queens, my body began acting strange again, just like it had back at home. I didn't want to just sit still, so I got out of bed and started walking the halls of the psych ward, trying to shake it off. My head twitched, one side of my body felt stiff, and my words slurred as I passed by. Everyone watched. During my stay, I noticed a doctor who I thought was the head of the psych ward. I asked the nurses if I could speak with him, but they told me he wouldn't be back until morning.

When morning came, I realized he wasn't the head doctor at all, he was just the physician, a kind, elderly Indian doctor who actually listened. The real head doctor came later, along with my psych doctor. Compared to the physician's warmth, the head doctor was cold and stern. He ordered me into a meeting room. I told him I didn't like my psych doctor because she never listened to me. His face tightened with anger.

"She'll be joining us one way or another," he snapped.

Inside the room, he looked at me and said, "The nurses told me you had a reaction to the medicine."

"It wasn't a reaction," I told him.

He rolled his eyes. "I know people like you. You lie and make things up just to get out of here early."

"Why would I lie?" I shot back.

"I'm leaving tomorrow anyway." When the meeting ended, and it was just my psych doctor and me, I turned to her and said,

"I'm lying? This slur is fake, huh?"

She just nodded silently. "No."

I was furious. How could a doctor say such things to a patient, let alone the head doctor? On the hospital walls were posters with hotlines for filing complaints. That's exactly what I did. I called the number, explained what happened, and the man on the phone was shocked. He apologized on the hospital's behalf, and for the first time that week, I felt a little peace. The next morning, my last day, I woke up excited to go home. But my twitching came back, worse than before, every second. I walked down the hall toward the nurses' station to check the time, and then I collapsed. When I came to, my nurse and the physician stood beside me. They told me I'd had a seizure. They sent me downstairs for observation. I must have fallen asleep on the hospital bed, because when I woke up, another doctor said I was fine and cleared me to go home.

If you ever need to file a complaint against a hospital in New York, here are the numbers I called: New York State Office of Mental Health: 1-800-597-8481 New York State Department of Health: 1-800-804-5447

Chapter 47 - Elon Musk

I believed Elon Musk was communicating with me through the TV and my son's tablet. I thought he knew I was the chosen one. That he would come pick me up and together we'd save the world. One night, I was sure we were supposed to meet. I felt like he was sending messages through my son's tablet. So, I sat outside my house, convinced the cops were watching, and that all I had to do was whistle. Suddenly, cars started moving, and then a minivan pulled up and the sliding door opened. I stood there, staring at the empty seat inside, torn , should I get in or not? I was certain that ride would take me to Elon Musk, where we'd talk through my struggles and find a way to fix the world. But in the end, I decided not to go.

Chapter 48 - Lil Wayne

I believed Lil Wayne was an oracle who knew about my coming.

Because we both suffered from childhood trauma, I felt we shared a spiritual connection. My third hospitalization happened after I was handcuffed for sitting in the middle of the street. My husband said I wasn't mentally present at the time. I had no idea what was really happening, all the stories I created, the visions and connections, felt like fragments of another reality. I thought I was being sent away because my husband called missing persons when I told him I was leaving him for good. It's a long story, but the hospital I was taken to was supposedly the psychiatric hospital Kanye West secretly took over.

There was a woman named Heather Grey, a famous public defender who had worked in hospitals for years. I believed she was a psychiatrist who met Lil Wayne when he was a child. He had told her about his visions of a new world. It reminded me of Harley Quinn, a doctor before she became who she is. I thought Heather Grey created Valeria to find me and use my X-Men-like powers to heal the world through my prayers. Lil Wayne knew all this because he had the "white eye", half blind, with visions that came and went just like his eyes. He was the oracle. I remember being in the harsh emergency waiting rooms, getting a shot, and as my eyes closed, I heard Lil Wayne's song playing loudly in the background.

Chapter 49 - H and Helicopters

There was a 21-year-old boy I met who I believed was sent by the police to protect me and eventually escort me out. His favorite phrase was, "these days." He was quiet, didn't say much, but often sat by the window with me as we listened to music on our headphones. One night, he said, "Yeah, you know, like being chased by cars and helicopters." The night I was hospitalized, I was trying to walk to Montauk but was also avoiding cops and helicopters. I was so exhausted by their rules and control.

I wanted to join the gifted community on my own terms. I felt like every second was a test, and I hated it. If they wanted me, they'd have to come to me. At one point, I even hid in the woods, imagining army men lying in wait for me, but I wasn't ready. I walked on, pretending I was about to throw myself off a bridge. I even sat in the middle of the road, tired of constantly fighting off cops and helicopters that followed me everywhere. One night, as we gathered around a table, H looked at me and said, "Isn't it time we had a new leader?" I just nodded and said, "Yes."

Chapter 50 - UFO

On my countertop sits an oversized baby bottle sterilizer from Korea, its shape and color so pretty, I don't mind that it takes up space. But it requires a Korean outlet, and not just any weak one. So my husband bought this bulky transformer to plug it in. One day, while I wasn't feeling well, having seizures and caught in a low- grade mania where I felt quietly hyper and excited about every moment, my husband was taking care of our son. He left out a white cutting board and a few utensils: a kitchen knife, a ladle, tongs, and metal chopsticks. To me, those utensils looked like they were all pointing at the transformer.

In my mind, I believed he placed them there intentionally to help send my frequency waves out into space. I thought he knew I was a special entity, and that he and a select few were part of the secret. But that fantasy only lasted seconds before fading away, as if the thought never happened, and I didn't need to look back. I also thought of the Helix Nebula, which looks like an eye in outer space, and believed that eye was connected to me. I truly felt I was a special entity, and even the CIA knew about it. I even protested that I was "an it" in the psych ward, writing notes on paper that said "Area 51".

Chapter 51 - Platform 9¾

There was a young woman I met during my hospitalization who made the whole experience feel... magical. The same woman who once said to me, "Google me, bitch." One of the strangest, most magical parts? Before I even entered the hospital, I had said something eerily similar to my doctor. I told him to look me up online. To see my digital footprint, to prove that I was stable. That I had a life. A career. A presence. And then, inside the ward, I meet this woman who boldly says to everyone: "Google me, bitch." She was like a mirror, reflecting back the part of me that wanted to be seen, but didn't know how to say it without being punished for it.

She left little notes everywhere, messages scrawled on scraps of paper that said things like, "We leave here at 3." "This place is a concentration camp." We even tried to break free once, tried to kick open the locked doors like we were escaping from some dystopian movie. One day, she turned to me and said, "I can't watch TV anymore. I feel like it's all about me." And I felt that, on every level.

There was a show premiering at the time, one called Naomi, about a girl who discovers she has the power to move the wind. An angel appears. A mystery unfolds. It just so happened to premiere on my birthday. I thought the directors were oracles, that they knew I was becoming something else, something more. Like Jean Grey from X-Men, except without the flaming phoenix. I believed I had been chosen, gifted by ancient gods, the ones who sent birds to Earth on rays of sunlight. I wasn't just a patient. I was standing at my own Platform 9¾, waiting for the train to take me somewhere only the gifted could go.

Chapter 52 - Scrooge and the Third Eye

It was a week before Christmas, and the TV channels were playing holiday films on repeat. One evening, a patient gathered a group of us to watch her favorite movie: Scrooge with Bill Murray. We sat in the common room, ten of us lined up in silence, the glow of the TV flickering against the dull walls. Her favorite scene came on, the one where Bill Murray is dining at a restaurant and suddenly finds an eyeball floating in his glass of water. The patient burst into uncontrollable laughter. She screamed with delight, laughing so hard she couldn't stop. The rest of us just stared at each other, unsettled. What the heck is going on? For me, it felt different. The scene didn't just play on the TV; it played for me. It was as if the universe had slipped a secret message into the movie, a reminder that I was connected to something greater. Watching that eyeball float in the glass, I felt my third eye had opened.

Chapter 53 - PBA

You know how, in the movie Joker, he couldn't control his laughter? I didn't realize that was based on a real condition, until it happened to me. For two days, I couldn't stop myself. The laughter would rise up out of nowhere, at the wrong times, in the wrong places. I tried to swallow it, force it back down, but it slipped through anyway. It's called the Pseudobulbar Effect.

Chapter 54 - Dalai Fucking Lama

There's a book called The Wisdom of Compassion by Victor Chan. I don't know why, but I randomly bought some psychology books, and one of them happened to be about Chan's friendship with the Dalai Lama. In one part, Chan watches a recording of the Dalai Lama's meeting and meditation. The way he described him made me feel like we were twins. I used to be super giggly and bubbly all the time, until I woke up. And then woke up again, realizing my life had been so good, but I was chasing some kind of fantasy... or maybe it was chasing me. In the book, Chan says that as soon as the Dalai Lama began to meditate, the recording suddenly shut off. He tried everything to recover it, but it was just gone.

A month after reading that, I started believing I could communicate with him through meditation. I thought I could poltergeist my thoughts into technology and connect directly with the Lama himself. I told my friend, who was a patient at the time, "He knows exactly who I am, and he can suck my dick." There's also a chapter where Chan asks the Dalai Lama about worldly problems, and the Lama just giggles. Looking back, during my grandiose phase, I thought the Lama was chill because he already knew the answers would be solved, through me.

Chapter 55 - Pocahontas

One day, I sat by the window, mesmerized by the wind and the rustling leaves dancing in the breeze. I felt deeply connected, one with nature and the weather. I believed I was linked to the living and the dead, smiling at the spirits carried by the wind. Every moment felt purposeful, even the birds flying by. As I stared into the spirits, a voice came from behind me, saying, "What's up, Pocahontas?" I turned to see who it was, wondering how she knew my name. She began to dance, full of energy, moving with everything she had, and I was amazed.

Then she braided my hair, like we were preparing for battle. Moments later, she took off my headphones and told me she was connected to the radio, like, literally connected. She switched the station to 105.1, explaining they were less mainstream and didn't take money. In that moment, I believed she could telepathically link to the radio, but with powers even greater, able to connect with Funkmaster Flex himself. One day she asked me, "You have powers too, right? It's been so long since I used mine. But you're the ninth power, you see, I'm the eighth. You're a high priestess."

Chapter 56 - Mrs. Daisy

There was an elderly lady I met who had the sweetest voice. As the weeks went by, she barely left her room or even ate. One day, I went to check on her, and she quietly said, "We have a lot of missions, don't we?" I stepped back and nodded, because all I wanted was to get out of the hospital as soon as possible and be with my son. I eventually believed my son and I were being protected from those who sought infinite knowledge for themselves, to use it selfishly. I thought the popes were coming for me, to declare me a high priestess. I imagined my son and me traveling the world, delegating tasks to shape the future. I believed it was the dawn of a new world order.

Chapter 57 - Fountain of Youth

Before my psychosis, before the crash, before the world inside my mind split open, I had a small dream buried in an old LLC I created years earlier, Nobull.life. It started as a clothing brand, then shifted into a consulting idea, and eventually became a little blog where I tried to write my way into healing. I wanted to help people, I wanted to create something honest, I wanted to make meaning out of my pain. One of the topics I planned to write about was the fountain of youth. I never published it, partly because the idea lived only in my head, and partly because I got sick before I ever had the chance.

But during my manic episode, the idea didn't just return; it came alive. I remember being at my parents' house, my mom and my stepdad, though we've never called him that. He's been "Dad" since the fourth grade, the real kind of dad, not the biological kind. They were sitting at the table eating dinner, just a normal night in our little universe. I was talking to them, moving in and out of my own thoughts, when suddenly their faces... changed. In front of me, they looked young; not slightly younger, not softened by dim lighting, but youthful, like they had been frozen in their early thirties. Smooth skin, bright eyes, faces untouched by time. It was so vivid and so real that I talked to them as if nothing unusual was happening. It didn't even occur to me to question it. Then, in a blink, a literal blink, their real faces snapped back into place. The wrinkles returned, the age, the years of life lived. I stared, confused for a moment, and then went right back to talking, because my brain was too far gone to understand what I had just seen.

Later, when the episode consumed me, I became convinced I had discovered the fountain of youth; that I had seen something holy; that I had unlocked a secret. To me, the answer was simple: Love, happiness, innocence, purity. I thought those were the ingredients that kept people young. Now I know it wasn't magic, it wasn't revelation, it was a hallucination. But even now, part of me still believes something in that moment was trying to teach me something; that maybe youth doesn't come from the body, but from the parts of us that stay soft, hopeful, and unbroken.

Chapter 58 - The Universe Speaking to Me: Hallucinations and the Hamptons

My first hallucination happened in the kitchen with my friend. We were about to head to the Hamptons when I noticed my moth traps, all filled with moths, beginning to move their wings. Earlier that week, the way the moths had landed had caught my attention. There was one single moth at the top, facing upward, and a cluster of dead moths beneath it. But it looked as if they were all facing that top moth. It might sound strange, but it reminded me of Jesus. This was right before my first hospitalization in 2019. I went in because I couldn't speak on command, I was having seizures, and my body was behaving unpredictably. Even now, I find myself staring at the pantry moth traps every time I wash my hands. I wonder, will they flap their wings like that again? Or will they form that strange pattern, like a silent vision of Jesus?

Chapter 59 - Durga Goddess: Worshiping the Moon and the Sun

During my psychosis, there was a moment in the kitchen when a shadow caught my eye. It looked like an ancient warrior's mask, a symbol of strength and protection. I believed it was a gift from the universe, my birthright earned through walking miles like a monk, living a disciplined, intentional life. This, I felt, was my reward. I found solace gazing at the sky, feeling deeply connected to the moon and the drifting clouds above. Usually in the psych ward, I danced quietly by the windows at the end of the hall near the garages, where no one could see me. But one day, sunlight poured perfectly into my room. I pulled out a chair and danced as if I were in a studio, delighting in the way my shadow twirled and dipped with me. Flipping through the channels, I landed on a Spanish radio station, where the hosts were cheering and celebrating. I believed they were cheering because I had chosen their station. So, I danced along with them, imagining they were watching me, impossible, yet at the time, that was my truth: I, the gifted one, had chosen their music to move to.

Chapter 60 - Mission: Africa

I don't know exactly why, but I've always felt a deep emotional pull toward Africa. Maybe it's ancestral. Maybe it's spiritual. Maybe it's just the truth of being human. But what I do know is this: The world owes Africa. Its people. It's land. Its soul. During my inpatient stay, I would sit by this giant window every day. Something about it felt sacred. It became my altar. I believed I was working undercover with the police, communicating in secret, through music, through body language, through signs only we could understand.

They were waiting for me to be released. Until then, they were protecting me. I believed some of the other patients were placed there too, undercover, like me. Helpers. Guides. One woman told me, "I called my friend from the police and said we were already speaking in code through the music." That line never left me. Because I was already living in code, feeling the messages beneath the surface of every song, every gesture, every glance. Another woman arrived shortly after. Quiet. Watchful. She had a habit of drifting into other people's rooms like she was looking for something lost. One afternoon, she yelled from the bathroom, "I have a weapon. Don't come near me." When she emerged, it was just books in her hand. Books. As weapons. That made sense to me. Her name was Liz. And in my eyes, she was part of the task force, an agent just like me.

I saw signs everywhere: books left open to specific pages, symbols drawn on notepads, eyes locked for a little too long. It all meant something. We weren't just patients. We were the chosen ones, placed on assignment. I'd sit by that window, listening to the radio, and start using American Sign Language to send messages to the world outside. To the cars passing, to the staff, to the sky. I signed things like:

"SEND ALL WHITE TO AFRICA" "WEED IS THE ANSWER" I believed the Uber drivers, the taxis, the visitors were all government operatives waiting on orders. And me? I was the Oracle. High Priestess of a new world order. The one who would bring healing. Clarity.

Truth. I truly believed weed was God's medicine, sent to cure the diseases man created. Cancer of the body, cancer of the earth, cancer of the soul. It made sense to me. I had seizures, vertigo, and narcolepsy, and no one had answers. But I did. And I began using one sign over and over again, "F" across my chest. To the world, it was just a letter. To me, it was everything. F for the Phoenix. My fire. My rebirth. My role. And then there was that girl again, the one who once called me Pocahontas. One day, she stared deep into me and said: "You're a high priestess, right? I haven't used my powers in a long time, but damn... I'm the eighth power. You're the ninth." And in that moment, it all clicked. Africa. The Phoenix. The Mission. Everything. Even if the world couldn't see it, I could. And for a moment, that was enough.

Chapter 61 - Rihanna the Oracle and the Hellsinger

In November, Rihanna was honored as a national hero in Barbados. I remember watching a clip of her walking up the stairs, moving with such grace, and for a moment, her eyes looked like mine, eyes of the divine. I believed she had been anointed not just for her fame, but for her songs. "Needed Me" had saved me during my darkest hours; I sang it over and over again, clinging to its strength like a lifeline. I thought she was an Oracle, a woman who somehow knew her voice would one day save a child like me. During this time, I couldn't always speak on command. My words would get stuck, trapped inside me. So, I turned to music, training my voice and my speech through song. The more I sang, the more I began to believe I was a Hellsinger, someone whose voice had been forged to fight evil, to cast it out. I was so desperate to help save the world, to let my voice be heard, that I even signed up for a singing competition. I recorded a video audition and sent it in, convinced that this was how my destiny would begin.

Chapter 62 - Phoenix and the Universe

In those days, I believed the universe was speaking to me through the birds. Their calls weren't just sounds, they were messages, and signs guiding me forward. I thought the Phoenix had blessed me, had granted me gifts beyond comprehension. In my state of psychosis, that belief felt undeniable, like destiny unfolding in real time. One night, when words failed me, I picked up a marker and drew a phoenix on the wall. Speaking had become nearly impossible; my voice tangled somewhere between silence and struggle. But the image was my way of showing my husband that this wasn't madness, it was a transformation.

Chapter 63 - Rome Was Built in a Day

I faced so much racism and abuse from doctors that I truly believed I would be able to sue them. My body had suffered, my conditions had worsened over time, and I had the proof. For a while, I thought that case would be my way forward, that with the money, I could finally build something better, not just for me but for everyone. I wanted to show the world that we deserve a life of dignity, that with justice and knowledge, things could change. But the truth hit me hard: those kinds of cases are nearly impossible to win. My hope slipped away as quickly as it had come.

When I was in god mode, my mind raced far beyond lawsuits and hospitals. I thought the world was about to flip into a new era, something out of The Hunger Games. I imagined humanity uniting against racism and oppression, a world where peace wasn't just a dream but a revolution we could touch. And in that same fevered vision, I had wild plans of justice. I thought that as the new world leader, I'd send all pedophiles and rapists to "Suicide Island" in Japan, where victims could hunt them down one by one. It was brutal, raw, and, in my mind at the time, perfectly fair. Pipe dreams, maybe. But they were mine.

Chapter 64 - Ancient Gods and Jesus

There's a music video by Ariana Grande called God Is a Woman. In it, there's a moment where she slams down a hammer like Thor and declares, "I will strike down on thee with furious anger." When I saw that, something clicked inside me. I thought I was vengeance itself, the fury of a goddess returned to earth. A spirit of wrath and justice, carrying the weight of centuries of pain. I burned with anger: anger at what the world had become, anger at the cruelty, the endless wars, not only between nations, but the quiet wars people fought within themselves every day. I believed it was my destiny to diminish evil, to burn it away. I thought I was chosen because I was the Phoenix, reborn from ashes, and impossible to destroy. I thought I was Constantine, the one destined to stand between good and evil.

Chapter 65 - Turning Water into Wine

Before my hospitalizations, I went through something I can only describe as my own version of Dante's Inferno. I would pass out, and when I did, it felt like my body was pinned under an immense, crushing weight. No matter how much I tried, I couldn't move. Inside my mind, it was as if I had to fight my way through the rings of hell, each stage darker and stranger than the last, like an episode of American Horror Story. Sometimes, when I finally broke through, I came out with an adrenaline rush so strong I felt unstoppable, almost superhuman. Other times, the aftermath was the complete opposite, I would wake up mute, unable to force out a single word, as if my voice had been stolen. My husband told me I was under immense stress during this period, and maybe he was right. But what made it even stranger was that when I drank a simple glass of water, I would feel tipsy, almost drunk. I kid you not, it was as if I was turning water into wine. In those moments, I felt like Jesus.

Chapter 66 - Malice

I hate talking about this because it still makes me want to cry, but I'm going to write it out. People need to know that abuse can happen in psychiatric hospitals, too. It was during my third hospitalization, at a psych ward in Queens.

In the early days, my eyes were in so much pain I kept passing out from it. I remember lying in my room, wrapping a shirt tightly around my eyes, desperate for relief. At one point, I went blind for a while and even had a seizure in my room. The pain was unbearable. One night, it got so bad I stumbled into the hallway, begging, begging, for someone to check my vitals. I needed to know what was happening. Why were my eyes burning like that?

There was a mental health worker who had been bullying me from the start. She once nearly shoved me, and even the other patients noticed. They asked if I was okay after seeing her aggression. Then there was the head night nurse, Lisa. I nicknamed her Malice. She always dressed up head-to-toe, even in scrubs she wore heels and bright red lipstick like the planet Mars. She reminded me of a twisted version of Alice in Wonderland. There was something about her energy: cold, dismissive, untouchable. Mal, bad. I don't remember what exactly triggered me that night, but I shouted, "WHO WANTS TO GET FIRED TODAY?"

I truly believed I was undercover at a special facility, maybe even Kanye West's, and that once my mission was done, I'd have the power to fire anyone who treated patients cruelly. Looking back, I know now I was severely unwell, but the fact that my distress triggered her response says something, doesn't it? Lisa would roll her eyes at patients' mid-seizure. Real or imagined, the girl collapsed and hit her head on the floor, and still, an eye roll.

That night, no one came to help me. No one checked my vitals. I remember hearing a staff member, Sandy, passing by. I don't know if it was real or imagined, but I swear I heard her mutter the word: "Malice."

Chapter 67 - The Judge's Words

I remember the day the judge said to me, "You're smiling too much." And just like that, my freedom was denied. In that moment, everything changed. My plans - once so clear - were shattered. I had dreamed of joining the National Guard part-time, or maybe working with the CIA. All so I could be with my son, to build a life for us. But the hospital stay dragged on, longer than I could bear. Being locked away that long, without my child tore at the edges of my mind. You don't just lose time there. You lose pieces of your reality, your sense of self. And no matter how much I smiled, how much I tried to hold on, the hospital was breaking me.

Chapter 68 - The Pain That Broke the Spell

It wasn't until the second week that the magic started to wear off. Not because I stopped believing in signs or secret programs or phoenixes, but because I couldn't go home. I missed my son so badly it ached through my bones. Up until that point, I had kept myself busy, decoding messages, making meaning from chaos, feeling like the universe had a plan for me. But then the silence crept in. And reality hit hard. No matter how chosen I believed I was... No matter how magical the ward felt... I was still a mother, and I was still missing bedtime kisses and tiny hands on my face. It killed me to count the days. Because every day away from him felt like a betrayal I couldn't undo.

Chapter 69 - Severe Depression

I kept my hopes up in the hospital, clinging to the idea that I'd be released soon, so I could see my son and continue on the path I believed was my destiny. But when the court ordered me to take medication, everything changed. My stay was extended by almost three more agonizing weeks. I missed my son more than words can express. I avoided calling at first because I knew just hearing his voice would break me.

When I finally learned about video calls two weeks into my stay, I tried, but each call shattered me. I couldn't stop crying. All I wanted was to hold him again. I was gone for one month and three days. That kind of absence isn't just painful; it's torture for a mother. It's a pain that no physical pain can compare too. The aching and longing in your mind and body... It doesn't just leave now that I'm out,

I'm grateful every day that I get to be with him again. I still have dreams of working, of building something meaningful. But for now, being his mother is the most important job in the world, and nothing comes before that. In the midst of the fog, when time felt broken, and I wasn't sure what was real, there was one nurse who felt... different. Not just kind, but present. Like his spirit hadn't been dulled by the sterile white walls or the weight of watching so many people fall apart. I don't remember what I said to him exactly; my mind was slipping in and out of itself, but something in me recognized something in him. And I told him. He smiled softly, and said, "Someone close to me once told me I'm going to make a difference one day." And without hesitation, I said, "You already are." I meant it.

With every cell of my broken, aching heart, I knew he was one of the good ones. The kind of person who helps without needing recognition. Who stands steady in a storm. But then I slipped again. I told him I was the reincarnation of the Virgin Mary. Maybe that was the moment he decided I was gone.

Chapter 70 - When My Mind Betrayed My Heart

Psychosis doesn't just make you lose touch with reality. Sometimes, it twists the very things you love the most. Sometimes, it pulls you toward people you should've left in the past. Sometimes, it makes you believe destiny is calling when it's really delusion whispering in your ear.

During my episode, I was convinced the universe was speaking directly to me. Every thought felt like a message. Every feeling felt like a sign. And one of those signs told me to reach out to someone from my past. An ex. It didn't feel like a choice, it felt like purpose, like fate, like a cosmic assignment I couldn't ignore. I thought he was the only one who understood me, not because he actually did, but because I believed the entire world was against me, except him. So, I texted him. And texted him. And texted him, fully convinced the universe wanted us to reconnect.

Meanwhile, the real universe, the one with gravity and logic and love, was standing right in front of me, watching his wife slip away. My husband. He watched me laugh at messages he never saw. He watched me hide the phone he paid for. He watched me, the woman he vowed his life to, reach for someone else in a moment that wasn't truly mine. It broke him. Shattered him in ways that still hurt to think about. But he didn't yell, he didn't leave, he didn't throw our life away. He just waited, terrified, confused, hurting, but waiting for me to come back. And the truth is painful but simple: I would NEVER leave him in a healthy mind. Not in this world. Not in any reality where I am myself. The only world where I almost lost him was the one my psychosis invented. And then it happened again, another spiral, another wave of delusion, another moment where my illness convinced me that destiny was pulling me toward a different life. But destiny wasn't doing anything, delusion was. My husband stayed anyway. When I finally recovered, really recovered,

I asked him the question that had been sitting in my throat like a stone: "Why did you stay? When I put you through all of that pain...

why did you stay?"

He looked at me, soft and steady and heartbreakingly simple, and said, "You don't remember our vows? Till death do us part."

And that was the moment I realized: Mental illness may have shaken our marriage, but love, real love, held the foundation steady until I could stand on it again.

Chapter 71 - My Significant Other

I was away for a month and three days, institutionalized, and even then, I didn't realize how much was still going on in my head. Two weeks after I got out, I almost forgot the mania entirely and remembered only my son. I was so eager, so mad at the system, because I seemed 100% normal on the outside. No one knew my thoughts, no one knew I believed I was receiving messages to go out and save the world. It wasn't constant, but now it feels like it consumes every day, every second. How does one simply forget that a fantasy was actually happening? During that month, I hated him, my husband so much. I was cruel on the phone when I finally started calling him. "I hate you," I said. "You put me here because you called missing person." In my manic mind, I had already decided to leave him, to divorce him, because I physically recoiled whenever he stood near me. It felt like natural law, our story prewritten.

My mind wove this intricate tale: our mothers were sent from Korea; we were destined to be together; our lives mapped out down to street numbers and angel numbers. He was born to father my child, but he knew our time together would be temporary, that I was meant to blossom into an Oracle. One day, an app advertisement for a game appeared on my phone, a game about a wife leaving her husband and child to build a fortress and save the world. At that moment, I thought those were my choices: divorce him or keep him and have him help raise our son. I don't know where it all started. I just woke up one morning, and the stories kept unfolding while real life carried on.

One day, my neighbor upstairs, pushing her laundry stroller, glanced around and asked, "You're not doing this for the news or TV shows, are you?" I just froze. What the actual fuck. That question captured my fractured reality. I hoped I'd never wake up again to a déjà vu, to my thoughts running wild. Being out socially feels different now. I don't feel normal. I hope someday I can look back and laugh, because laughter is key in life. Life is a paradox; you just have to keep laughing. I learned that even when I had that uncontrollable laughing disorder, like the Joker's, I could internalize it in two days.

That's strength. Magic, if you will. Deep inside the psych ward, I hated my husband with a fierceness I didn't recognize. I cursed him after our son went to bed, blaming him for everything, especially for putting me there. I was convinced destiny had shifted, I needed to leave him behind. The idea gripped me so tightly I couldn't see past it. But outside those walls, my father-in-law told him to leave me, to walk away from a woman lost in darkness. And he said no. "I love her," he said. It wasn't easy for him. He was overwhelmed, hopeless, unsure how to help. He sought therapy, a brave, deliberate choice that showed his desire to understand, to heal, and to stay. That simple sentence held a universe of meaning. He didn't run when it was easiest. He stayed through the storm, even when I pushed him away.

He carried the weight of our brokenness alongside me, and that loyalty changed everything. Looking back now, I see what real love is, not just passion or promise, but a choice to stand firm when everything else falls apart.

Chapter 72 - The Seer

One day, years before anything made sense, I was at a wedding with my husband. The music was loud, people were laughing, the room was full of movement and celebration. And then I saw her, his aunt, slowly making her way across the room toward me. She was already old back then. Her steps were careful. Her shoulders hunched. Her hands trembling with age. But her eyes... her eyes were clear. She reached me and gently placed both of her fragile hands on my arms. They were warm and shaking, but steady in intention. She held me there for a moment, just long enough to make me wonder what she saw. Then she said it, quietly, almost like a prophecy:

"You're gonna be someone someday." I remember giving her a small smile, a soft giggle, polite, dismissing it with the kind of disbelief you have when someone says something too big for you to imagine.

I walked away as if she never said it, as if her words weren't meant for me, as if a comment from an elderly woman was just that, a comment. But years later, in the psych ward, her voice found me again. Her words echoed inside the sterile walls, louder than the doctors, louder than the alarms, louder than the chaos in my head.

When everything else in my mind felt broken and scrambled, her voice was the one thing that cut through the noise. "You're gonna be someone someday." And sitting there on that hard hospital mattress, hair unwashed, mind unraveling, heart heavy with confusion, I whispered back to myself: "Yeah... a real star." Not with pride, not with humor, with disbelief, with pain, with the ache of someone who thought her life was ending, not beginning. Her words felt like a knife back then, a reminder of the person I was supposed to become, and how far away she seemed. But then came the memoir, the writing, the healing, the truth, the voice I didn't know I had. And eventually, the day my book was published. And something shifted. Her prophecy didn't hurt anymore. It didn't feel like pressure. It didn't feel like an impossible destiny I failed to reach.

It felt like strength, like a reminder, like a thread connecting who I was, who I became, and who I am still growing into. I used to think she saw a future version of me I could never live up to. Now I realize something better: She didn't see my success, she saw my spirit. And she was right. I am someone, and I'm still becoming

Chapter 73 - The End

No, it's not really the end, because I'm still here, slowly recovering, and I'm proud of myself for that. Amen to the Gods, then. My husband and I have reached a point in our relationship where we don't even need cute emojis anymore, our love runs deeper than that. And honestly, you'd never guess I went through all this if you met me. I've always been me, a loving, generous woman. At 35, whether you call it manic or spiritual, I don't think it was crazy. I thought it was beautiful. In the ward, I prayed. I meditated. I danced, until the pills slowed me down and I gained weight from it. That part sucked, but even then, I found my rituals. I'd lay my blanket on the floor under the giant window where the moonlight poured in, and I'd pray to the moon itself. Sometimes Natalie joined me. She was something else. We connected instantly, often sitting together in silence, but when words did come, it felt magical, like the universe had cracked open just for us. So no, this isn't the end. It's just another beginning.

Chapter 74 - Looking Back at Baby Jenn

I always wonder how different life would have been if my dad had never laid his hands on my mom. Maybe I wouldn't have grown into the spunky girl with a septum ring. Maybe New Jersey Jenn would have turned out softer, calmer, untouched by chaos. Without the manic episode, without all of it, who knows what version of me would be standing here now. I hope one day I can look back at all of this and laugh, turn it into a story I tell with a smirk instead of a sting. But right now, it still hurts. It hurts to know something like this happened to someone like me.

Just a regular woman who wanted a normal life. I hate my father for what he did, for every bruise and scream that haunted our home until my mom finally left him. She saved us from that hell. I thank her silently every day for her courage. My father? I have nothing for him. No feelings, no name. I couldn't even remember it when Social Security asked for it during my disability claim. And I didn't care to. I've been hospitalized three times now, and I'm not proud of it. The first two were for physical reasons. The third... that was different. That was when delusions of grandeur swallowed me whole. Sometimes, I miss who I used to be, the animated, happy-go-lucky version of myself. Now I feel like I'm just... going. But maybe that's okay. Maybe I'll flourish again or at least try to. And another thought: aren't we all crystal children in some way? Shards of something fragile, reflecting both light and fracture.

Chapter 75 - The Party

I remember it all too well. It was the summer of 2019, and I was lying on a stretcher in the hospital, waiting by the nurses' station. My mom and husband were somewhere, probably talking to doctors or amongst themselves about me. I stared at the ceiling, lost in my own thoughts, when the doctor approached and asked, "Did you know you're pregnant?" I yelled, "WHAT?!" so loud that even with my slurred speech, it came out crystal clear. My face went pale. I couldn't believe it, I was pregnant, and at a time like this. Looking back now, I understand that hypersexuality comes with bipolar disorder, and during my manic state, I had been hypersexual. I spent ten whole days in the psych ward, alone and scared. Luckily, there were a few patients I befriended, which helped me pass the time. But when night fell, the solitude crept in. I wasn't alone with anyone else, but I was alone with myself. I would hold my belly and cry. I sobbed because what kind of life was this? Pregnant in a psych ward... out of all places, a psych ward. Let that sink in. Usually, people share the news with family, throw parties, and celebrate with dinners. But me? I was in Hell.

Chapter 76 - Drugs

The court ordered me to take Lithium and Risperdal, or something like that. Now I'm only on Invega, and I hate it. I've gained over twenty pounds from these pills, and every time I look in the mirror, I feel disgusted with myself. I don't feel happy anymore. Every second feels forced. The only thing I look forward to is sleeping. I sleep a lot. Sometimes I nap during the day while my son plays in the apartment. That's the part that kills me, how checked out I've become. I despise every pound on my body, and I despise every wild story I created when I was manic. It came out of nowhere, swallowed me whole, and took months to crawl out of. Recovery feels endless, like dragging myself across broken glass. Invega is technically a drug for schizophrenia, but they said it helps with bipolar disorder, too. Honestly, I've never believed I was "bipolar." I spent weeks in hospitals with people who were, and they'll tell you themselves, I never had mood swings. People used to call me a monk. Calm, centered, steady. I was smiley, talkative, active. Now? I feel like I'm stuck in limbo, trapped in a body I don't recognize, cursed with weight gain and exhaustion. Even my husband admits I'm not spunky anymore. Maybe it's the pills. Maybe it's the crash after everything I went through, the brutal slap of reality after waking up from manic grandeur. That episode was terrifying. If I hadn't come back, maybe I'd be on the streets right now, holding up signs that say, "God is coming sooner than you think." Just another "crazy" homeless person. The thought frightens me. So maybe now the label fits: manic-depressive. My life feels like a loop. Wake up, same routine, same exhaustion, same naps. It's like being stuck in a never-ending vacation, but not the good kind. I can't work. I can barely be present. And I'm so embarrassed by what happened to me, even though no one else knows the full story. I do. I mean, I thought I was Lil Wayne's soulmate. I thought Eminem was some kind of oracle. And I was sober at the time. Sure, I hit the one- hitter occasionally but compared to how much weed I used to smoke before my son was born, I was basically clean. Back then,

I was a bartender, fast, busy, active. Now, I'm exhausted beyond words. I'm in the process of switching medications. The drug they have me on makes me oversleep and drags me into this fog. The doctor wants me to stay on the injection two more times while the new meds build up to the right level. My husband doesn't know. I'm sure he wouldn't approve. But I need to try. I need to see if I can find myself again, the happy-go-lucky girl, the funny one. The one who was still me.

Drug update: It's been almost four years since my psychotic episode, and now I'm on Vraylar. I feel alive again. I feel happier, no longer trapped in that zombie-like existence. It took me nearly four years to find the right medication, but finally, it works for me. I hope everyone struggling can find the treatment that helps them feel like themselves again.

Chapter 77 - "The Dance and the Goodbye"

Every day, I danced down the hospital hallways, spinning, shooting invisible guns, whispering numbers only I could hear. To the staff, I was a mystery, a storm they couldn't quite understand. But to me, it was survival. A way to hold onto myself when everything else felt like it was slipping away. On the day I was leaving, finally free, a nurse pulled me aside. Her eyes were gentle, tired. "You're like a movie star," she said softly. Not glamorous, not perfect. But someone who commands attention, who carries a story too heavy to ignore. There was sadness in her voice, for me, for all the battles no one saw. For the light in me that never dimmed, even in the darkest place. That moment, her words, felt like a benediction. A quiet acknowledgement that I survived. That I mattered. That maybe, somehow, I was meant for more than just these walls.

Chapter 78 - Psychosis

The mind is such a powerful thing. I slipped into psychosis twice, and both times it felt like my entire world turned upside down. I even questioned my relationship with my husband. I thought he was a spy, that everything in my life had been planned and orchestrated against me.

Coming back to reality was like waking from a nightmare. And there he was, my husband, patient, steady, welcoming me back with love, even though I had just put him through hell. If that's not proof that God exists, I don't know what is. During one manic stretch, I made an Instagram account, @seoulful_hippie. If you read those captions, you'll see the storm my mind was in. A part of me laughs at it now, but another part sees the pain behind every post. I wanted to save the world so badly that my mind snapped under the weight of it. A child psychologist once told me that my trauma and PTSD came back at me tenfold, exploding into seizures and physical illness. My closest friend, someone who's known me my entire life, believes it's years of unresolved trauma surfacing all at once. Maybe they're both right. Maybe it doesn't matter.

All I know is this: trauma doesn't just vanish. It waits. It festers. And if you don't face it, it finds a way to come back for you. That's why therapy, healing, and freeing yourself from the past are so important. And one more thing, my dreams? They're always about the apocalypse. Not because I believe the world is ending, but because, in a strange way, it's beautiful to me. Whole worlds collapsing in my sleep. Maybe that's just my minds way of telling it's still rebuilding'.

Chapter 79 - Psychosomatic Pain

I first learned about psychosomatic pain through ChatGPT. One day, while asking it to help refine parts of my memoir, the term came up. Psychosomatic pain, physical symptoms influenced by psychological factors like anxiety, stress, or unresolved emotional issues. When I realized this, I began to cry. All this time, I had been hurting, experiencing real physical pain, and no one had come to help. No one had offered answers. I had assumed it was all part of my psychosis, that I had imagined every ache, every throb. But learning that my pain was real, that my body was literally responding to the weight of my mind, broke me. It made me so angry. And I decided to turn that anger into something productive: writing. Writing became my way to help others who felt hurt and broken like me, wandering through life with no answers. I began to write a comic book, transforming my pain into something other than suffering, a way to tell my story, to channel the chaos, and maybe, in the process, help others feel seen. And hopefully this memoir will help others.

Chapter 80 - When the Mind Makes Its Own Truth

Psychosis doesn't just twist thoughts. It rewrites reality. When you're inside it, everything feels real, more real than memories, more real than logic, more real than anything anyone can tell you. Psychosis can make you believe things that never happened, fear things that weren't there, and react to a world only you can see. It doesn't mean you're dramatic. It doesn't mean you're weak. It doesn't mean you're broken. It means your brain was trying to survive in the only way it knew how.

During my episode, I believed things with my whole chest, things that now make no sense, things that feel wild to say out loud. But back then? They weren't "delusions." They were truth. They were certainty. They were the world as my mind presented it to me. That's what people don't understand: psychosis isn't choosing to believe something ridiculous, it's being trapped inside a reality that feels completely, painfully real. And coming out of it? That's the hardest part, because you have to walk backward out of a dream that wasn't a dream, a whole world collapsing behind you. But that doesn't make me dangerous. That doesn't make me unstable. It makes me someone who survived a war inside her mind, and lived to tell the story.

Chapter 81 - What's Normal?

My seizure-like episodes began when I was between 21 and 24, then returned with a vengeance in 2022, just before my second and third hospitalizations. Every EEG, MRI, blood test, and lab report came back normal. But there was nothing normal about the way my body was behaving. Eventually, I learned it was PNES, Psychogenic Nonepileptic Seizures, sometimes called functional seizures. The episodes look like epileptic seizures, but they aren't caused by abnormal electrical activity in the brain. Instead, they're linked to psychological stress and trauma, PTSD, depression, anxiety, dissociation, the body's unconscious response to overwhelming emotion. For years, hospital staff made me feel like my seizures were fake. Once, I was brought into the ER and left waiting by the entrance. An EMT kept pinching my arms, over and over, demanding I "wake up." The next day, I woke up covered in bruises. I'm relieved to finally have a name for what was happening, but the neglect I went through left me with physical challenges I couldn't explain. My body had gone into survival mode. Years of stress, mental strain, and physical neglect pushed me past my breaking point.

My nervous system had only three options: fight, flight, or freeze. And I refused to freeze. When my eyes hurt so badly, I thought I was going blind, I trained myself to live without sight. I memorized the placement of every piece of furniture in my apartment. I walked outside with my eyes closed, mapping the courtyard by feel, refusing to let fear make me helpless. When my voice stopped working, I taught myself sign language. Whatever my body took from me, I found another way. I studied what was happening, not just to survive, but because I knew one day I'd use it to help others heal. And maybe that was my magic all along, the gift of transforming struggle into strength, and suffering into something meaningful.

Chapter 82 - The Knowing

I've always known something was coming. Even before the hospital.

Before the breakdowns. Before I started seeing visions I couldn't explain and feeling things I couldn't describe. I didn't have a name for it, but I could feel it like a static charge in my chest. Like I was walking through life with an invisible string pulling me toward something... huge. Holy. Terrifying. It wasn't always dramatic.

Sometimes it was just a flicker, like déjà vu that lasted a little too long. Like hearing a lyric and feeling like it was written just for me, by something ancient. Like seeing strangers on the street and knowing I'd seen them before... even though I hadn't. As a child, I thought I was just sensitive. As an adult, I thought I was just anxious. Later, the world would call it a psychotic break. But deep down? It always felt like the moment I'd been bracing for. It didn't come all at once. The unraveling was slow at first. Little things. A voice here. A vision there. Dreams that felt like warnings. I'd walk into a room and feel like someone had just screamed, even if no one had spoken. I'd hold my son and feel a love so big it cracked something open inside me, like a portal. Then one day it was everywhere. My thoughts no longer belonged to me.

The veil between this world and the next was paper-thin, and I kept tearing through it. And instead of asking, "What's happening to me?" I remember thinking: "It's finally starting." People told me I was losing my mind. And maybe I was. But part of me knew, I wasn't just breaking. I was opening. To what, I didn't fully understand yet. But something in me believed I was being shown things, visions, signs, symbols, that mattered. That weren't just random noise. That maybe, just maybe, I was here for a reason beyond what any doctor could diagnose or explain. And when the pills numbed it, I felt something else die inside me: That sense of sacred urgency. That Knowing. But even when it faded, it never fully left. It stayed there, beneath the fog. Waiting for me to remember again. Looking back now? I think the Knowing was my first connection to God. Or at least... something bigger than me. It wasn't kind. It wasn't soft. It didn't promise answers. But it was real. More real than anything this world could offer me. And that's what kept me alive. Not the hospital. Not the medicine. But the feeling that this story wasn't over. That what I went through had meaning. That I was here to say something, once I survived it. I don't have all the answers. I still wrestle with doubt, fear, and disbelief. But one thing hasn't changed: I still know. Even when it hurts. Even when I forget. Somewhere deep inside, I've always known.

Chapter 83 - The Lightness

I don't have all the answers. I'm still broken in places. Still healing in others. But I've learned something sacred along the way: You don't have to be perfect to be whole. You don't have to have it all figured out to be enough. The weight I carried for so long, the confusion, the silence, the fear, it's lifting. Like a butterfly finally letting go of the heavy shell it once crawled from. And in that lightness, I'm starting to believe, not just in what's coming, but in myself. That's enough. That's everything. Reflection: If you've ever felt lost, broken, or unseen. know that your story matters. Your lightness is waiting to emerge, even in the darkest moments. Hold on to hope. You're not alone.

I Am the Architect of Alchemy: I've survived pains most can't name, and I've transformed them into a love language. A way to speak to the hurting. A way to remind people they're not alone. A way to help them breathe again. I'm not a god. I'm human. I carry the pain and the scars of a wounded soldier. I am not perfect. I am not healed. But I am healing. I am here. I am a survivor. I am still dancing. And that... is enough. Rules to live by:

Thou shalt feel deeply and not be punished for it.

Thou shalt question what they call real.

Thou shalt fall apart and rise differently.

Thou shalt honor the fire inside, even if it burns everything.

Thou shalt not betray thy soul for comfort.

Thou shalt name thy pain and listen to it.

Thou shalt not fear visions, they are guides in disguise.

Thou shalt protect the child within at all costs.

Thou shalt not be silent about truth, even when it shakes the room.

Thou shalt remember, you are not crazy. You are the echo of something ancient.

Chapter 84 – The Beginning

I'm writing a comic book now. It's kind of wild to think about, turning all the crazy stuff I've been through into pictures and words. Each page is like a piece of me. This comic isn't just a story. It's my way of taking back control and making something from all the pain and confusion. I hope when people read it, they see themselves in it and don't feel so alone. As this book ends, my comic is just beginning. It's the next part of my journey, louder, brighter, and real in a whole new way.

Chapter 85 - The Multiverse Inside Me

People say Rome wasn't built in a day. And honestly… I tried. I wanted to build everything at once, a story, a world, a purpose, a meaning for the pain I had lived through. I wanted to turn my trauma into architecture, my visions into bricks, my chaos into something beautiful. But instead of building Rome in a day, I ended up creating a multiverse in a week. It didn't begin as a comic. It began as survival. After my psychosis, when the world felt too loud and too quiet at the same time, my brain was still glowing with pieces of imagery, scenes, metaphors, symbols, memories, and half-truths that came from somewhere deep inside me.

I couldn't hold all of it in my mind without drowning, so I started writing. Not planning. Not outlining. Just… pouring. For seven days straight, I wrote like something inside me had cracked open. The words didn't feel like invention; they felt like recognition. The story didn't come from brainstorming; it came from remembering. That's how Divine Reckoning, The War Within was born. I wasn't trying to make a comic. I was trying to make sense of myself. At first, I didn't even name the main character Jenn. I almost named her Kina.

It sounded mystical, strong, symbolic, everything I wished I could be. But after a while, I realized something important: Why would I write a whole universe and not put myself at the center of it? This story was mine. This power was mine. This reckoning was mine. So "Kina" faded, and the real protagonist stepped in, the me who lived through psychosis, the me who felt everything too deeply, the me who fought her way out of darkness, the me who survived. Jenn became the heart of the comic. Not the flawless version of me. Not the heroic version. Just the true one, the one who carries scars, visions, rage, softness, grief, and hope all in the same body. The story grew quickly, faster than I could have imagined. In seven days I had pages and pages of scenes, ideas, characters, powers, symbols, and entire realities that didn't exist a week before. It was like my mind finally had somewhere safe to put the things it couldn't say out loud. People ask me how I wrote a multiverse so quickly. But the truth is… I didn't create it from scratch. It was already inside me. All I did was open the door. Seven days.

That's all it took to transform my pain into something with purpose.

Seven days to turn the darkest parts of my life into something meaningful. Seven days to rewrite my suffering into strength. I couldn't build Rome in one day. But I built a universe in seven. And maybe that's because the universe I needed most was the one where I finally became the main character of my own story.

I'm officially looking for a comic artist to collaborate with on a 60/40 partnership. If you want to see the story and scripts before applying, you can read them on my Patreon: patreon.com/seoulfulhippie. This project means the world to me, and I'm hoping to find an artist who believes in it just as much.

Chapter 86 - Bipolar Mukbang

If someone told me a year ago that people on TikTok would start recognizing me for drinking coffee and taking my morning antipsychotic on camera, I would've laughed. But here we are.

It started one morning when I opened the app before my brain fully woke up. I had my coffee in one hand, my pill in the other, and I thought, you know what? Let me just show the real routine. The real bipolar morning. No shame, no hiding, no pretending. So, I propped up my phone, took a sip of coffee, swallowed my antipsychotic, and hit "post" on my little corner of TikTok, @seoulfulhippie. No special lighting. No fancy editing. Just me, my coffee, and my reality.

And here's the thing: I don't have a huge following. I'm not viral-famous or brand-sponsored or anything shiny. But the people who do follow me? We've been lifting each other up in ways that feel real.

They cheer for my good days. I cheer for theirs. Some mornings we laugh together, some mornings we get vulnerable, and some

mornings we just show up, tired, messy, honest. And somehow, that became a community. Suddenly, my comments were full of:

"Thank you for normalizing meds." "This makes me feel less alone."

"I take mine with coffee too." "You make the mornings easier." And I realized: People didn't need another aesthetic routine. They needed someone who wasn't pretending. My bipolar mukbangs weren't a performance. They were a ritual. A grounding moment. A soft reminder that healing is sometimes nothing more than taking your meds with your morning coffee and choosing to stay. I never set out to build a community. But on @seoulfulhippie, that's exactly what happened, a small, gentle corner of the internet where we remind each other that surviving is worth celebrating. Coffee in hand. Camera on. Bipolar mukbang. And another day begins.

Chapter 87 - A Letter From My Husband

To anyone reading this, I want to share something from my side of the story. My wife has been brave enough to open her heart in these pages, and I want to honor her honesty with my own. Loving someone with bipolar disorder isn't always easy. But loving Jenn has never been hard.

There is a difference. When she went through psychosis, I watched the woman I loved slip into a world I couldn't see or understand. She laughed at things I couldn't hear, cried at things I couldn't fix, and looked at me like I was both a stranger and her only safe place at the same time. There were moments when I felt helpless. Moments I didn't know what to say. Moments I thought I was losing her.

Moments I was scared she was losing herself. People don't talk enough about the fear partners feel…the fear of not being enough, the fear of saying the wrong thing, the fear of watching someone you love fight a battle you can't step into. But even in the worst moments, even when it broke me to see her hurting, I remembered: We made vows in the presence of God. "To have and to hold from this day forward, for better, for worse, for richer, for poorer, in sickness and in health…" I meant them. All of them. She doesn't remember everything she said or did during her episode. But I remember the woman behind the symptoms.

The heart behind the confusion. The love behind the panic. The strength behind the illness. I held onto that. I want to speak directly to anyone who loves someone going through something similar: You are not alone. Your fear is valid. Your exhaustion is valid. Your frustration is valid. Your love matters more than you think. Be patient. Give grace. Learn what bipolar really is. Take care of yourself too. And when it feels scary, try to remember the person not the illness speaking through them. Recovery happens. Good days return. The laughter comes back. So does the light. Jenn is proof of that. Today, she is the strongest woman I know. Not because she never broke, but because she fought her way back and built a life filled with the kind of peace she never thought she'd feel again. I am proud of her. I am proud of this book. And I am proud to be the one beside her through everything … the storms, the healing, the rebuilding, and the life we have now.

To my wife: I love you. I'm glad you stayed. I'm glad we stayed. Thank you for letting me be part of your story. And to anyone reading this: Hold on. Love through it. Hope through it. There is life after the darkest days and you deserve to see it. Julius

Chapter 88 - One Piece

It's the smell that fills the house first, warm, sweet, freshly baked cookies drifting through the rooms like a reminder that love still lives here. Then comes the glow. The twinkling Christmas lights wrap our living room in a soft golden warmth, the kind childhood memories are made of. Every year, the weekend before

Thanksgiving, we put up our Christmas tree. It's our tradition, our way of choosing joy early. My husband lifts my son to the higher branches. My son hangs each ornament carefully, some crooked, some perfect. They laugh when one falls, fix it together, try again.

This year, I stepped away from the tree for a moment, just to take it in. The lights. The warmth. The peace filling our home. I sat back and simply… sat. Letting myself breathe. Letting myself feel the softness of a moment I once thought I would never get again.

Because there was a time when I wasn't here for any of this. I missed 54 days of my son's life when he was just two years old. Fifty-four days that I can never get back. A stretch of time where the world kept turning without me, holidays passing, routines shifting, memories forming in rooms I wasn't in. To anyone else, 54 days might not seem like much. But to a mother? Fifty-four days is a lifetime. For a long time, that number felt like a wound I carried quietly. But sitting on that couch, watching my husband and son decorate our tree, something inside me softened, something settled. I realized that those 54 days, as painful and irreplaceable as they were, do not define the mother I am today. They are not the stories my son will grow up remembering. They are not the ending. Because I can fill every year from now on with so much color, warmth, laughter, and love that those missing days become just one page in a long, beautiful story. And in that moment, I felt something I hadn't felt in years. Peace. The kind that doesn't shout. The kind that doesn't rush. The kind that arrives quietly and sits beside you like an old friend.

This is the piece of my life I once thought was lost forever, the piece I never imagined I'd get back, the piece that lets me close this book gently, with gratitude instead of grief. As the tree lit up in front of me, tiny stars glowing in our living room, I felt it all at once: I'm here. I'm whole. I'm home. And I finally have my one piece back, the one that brings me peace.

Acknowledgments

To everyone who has held a piece of my heart along this journey, thank you.

To my husband, Julius the steady one, the quiet strength behind every storm I survived. Thank you for loving me through the moments I couldn't love myself, for your patience when my world was loud, and for your faith when mine disappeared. You are the reason this book exists. You are the reason our family feels whole.

To my son my light, my softness, my reason. Thank you for giving me purpose in the darkest moments and joy in the smallest ones. Everything I do, everything I become, is for you.

To my mother for the sacrifices I only understand now as an adult, and for the strength I didn't realize I inherited.

To everyone who has walked with me through my mental-health journey my therapists, my doctors, the nurses who treated me with dignity, and the people who reminded me that bipolar is not a weakness but a way of navigating the world with deeper feeling. Thank you for seeing me as a whole human being, not an illness.

To my TikTok community @seoulfulhippie wouldn't exist without you. Thank you for showing up for my morning "bipolar mukbangs," for sharing your struggles, your victories, your stories. You made me feel less alone. You made me believe my voice mattered.

To every reader holding this book thank you. Thank you for giving my story a home inside your mind, for walking through the chaos and the beauty with me, and for choosing to understand instead of judge. I hope these pages remind you that healing is possible, even after the world breaks you open.

And finally, to the version of me who survived long enough to write this: I'm proud of you.

Final Reflection

If there is one thing I've learned from telling my story, it's that healing doesn't begin with answers. It begins with honesty. For most of my life, I carried pieces of myself in different rooms of my mind. Childhood fears locked away in one corner. Confusion in another. Moments I didn't understand. Memories I tried to outrun. Pain I minimized because I didn't know it counted. A version of myself I kept hidden because I didn't know she deserved to be seen.

Writing this memoir forced me to walk through those rooms one by one. Not as the broken girl I once was, but as the woman who survived her. I used to think strength meant pretending everything was fine. Now I know strength is saying, "This hurt me, and I'm still here." I used to think my story was too messy, too heavy, too complicated to share. Now I know that every messy part is a thread in the fabric of who I am. I used to think my bipolar disorder made me hard to love. Now I know it makes me love deeper, feel deeper, fight harder. I used to think the darkest moments defined me. Now I know they refined me.

If you are reading this and carrying your own heavy history, whether it's trauma, mental illness, heartbreak, confusion, or a childhood that still echoes in your bones, I hope you know this: You are not broken, you are becoming. Healing is not a straight line. It's a loop, a spiral, a circle that leads you back to yourself again and again. Some days you'll rise. Some days you'll fall. But every day you keep going is another day you win. I used to spend years wishing I could erase parts of my story. Now I see that every part served a purpose. Every hurt taught me something. Every loss made room for something new.

Every crack let the light in. This memoir isn't just about what happened to me. It's about who I became because of it. It's about choosing to stay. Choosing to heal. Choosing to write. Choosing to build a life that feels like peace, even after years that felt like chaos.

This is not the end of my story. But it is the chapter where I finally stop running from myself. If you're reading this and fighting your own battles, I hope you remember: You survive every single day you choose to keep going. And one day, maybe quietly, maybe suddenly, you'll look around and realize you're standing in a life you once prayed for, just like I did.

Epilogue

They said I was broken. Too emotional. Too dramatic. Too sensitive. Too much. They diagnosed me. Dismissed me. Charged me for care I didn't receive. Mocked my pain in rooms with white coats and no empathy. Told me to prove my seizures were real, as if my suffering was a stage performance. But the truth is, I wasn't broken. I was hungry. I was hurting. I was becoming. Becoming someone who now knows what a life without support feels like. Becoming someone who will spend the rest of her life making sure no one else feels that alone. This is bigger than me. I don't just want to share my story. I want to tear down systems that punish people for being sick. I want to build systems where healing doesn't require insurance or shame. Where you don't have to beg to be believed. Where survival isn't a luxury. I want free healthcare for everyone. Because healthcare is a human right. Not a privilege. Not a profit. Not a punchline from a doctor who doesn't see you as human.

Thank You! Every paperback purchased helps make a difference. For each copy sold, $1 is donated to Save the Children. Your support brings hope and healing to children worldwide.